SP

SINGER
UPHOLSTERY
Basics Plus

SINGER
UPHOLSTERY
Basics Plus

COMPLETE STEP-BY-STEP PHOTO GUIDE

STEVE CONE

Creative Publishing
international

Copyright © 2007
Creative Publishing international, Inc.
400 First Avenue North, Suite 300
Minneapolis, MN 55401
1-800-328-3895
www.creativepub.com
All rights reserved

Printed in China

10 9 8 7 6 5 4 3

Library of Congress Cataloging-in-Publication Data

Cone, Steve
  Singer upholstery basics plus : complete step-by-step
photo guide / Steve Cone.
    p. cm.
Includes index.
  ISBN-13: 978-1-58923-329-4 (soft cover)
  ISBN-10: 1-58923-329-8 (soft cover)
  1. Upholstery. I. Title.
TT198.C5 2007
  645'.4--dc22   2007007252

President/CEO: Ken Fund
Vice President/Sales & Marketing: Kevin Hamric
Publisher: Winnie Prentiss
Executive Managing Editor: Barbara Harold
Acquisition Editors: Linda Neubauer, Deborah Cannarella
Production Managers: Laura Hokkanen, Linda Halls

Creative Director: Michele Lanci-Altomare
Senior Design Manager: Brad Springer
Design Managers: Jon Simpson, Mary Rohl
Director of Photography: Tim Himsel
Lead Photographer: Steve Galvin
Photo Coordinator: Joanne Wawra
Book and Cover Design: Laurie Young
Page Layout: Laurie Young
Illustrator: Deb Pierce
Photographer: Joel Schnell

CONTENTS

INTRODUCTION

Upholstery is often a self-taught craft, learned by experimenting. With this approach, the only instructions for reupholstering a piece of furniture are developed while taking it apart. The obvious dilemma is that you must rely on the cleverness of the person who upholstered before you and risk repeating poor decisions. *Singer Upholstery Basics Plus* is designed to take the guesswork out of the upholstery process. Used as a guide, this book will help you recognize and repeat quality techniques, while avoiding unprofessional, and sometimes costly, errors.

Upholstery, when done well, can be very rewarding. Consider the creative satisfaction of returning a tattered cast-off to its like-new state, as well as the money saved because you didn't have to buy new. The comfort of a favorite chair need not be sacrificed simply because it no longer suits the color scheme of the room. Family heirlooms become more than cherished souvenirs when they are upholstered to blend with the décor of the home.

In the Getting Started section, acquaint yourself with the supplies, tools, and terms used for upholstery. Throughout this section, you will find detailed instructions for some of the most frequently required elements

in the upholstery process. Use this section as a reference for completing tasks such as stripping, webbing, tying springs, making cushions, and sewing skirts.

Whether your intent is to tackle one project or begin an ongoing hobby, set up a work space away from the general living area of your home. Depending on the amount of time you have available, projects can take several work sessions to complete. You will want to leave your project, supplies, and tools undisturbed between sessions.

The various furniture pieces in the Upholstery Projects section incorporate a full range of basic upholstery techniques for beginner to intermediate skill levels. This new, revised edition of *Upholstery Basics* includes five additional projects featuring popular furniture pieces. Acknowledging endless furniture design differences, it is likely that you may have to combine techniques from several projects to complete your particular piece. The process for upholstering an easy chair, for example, might include some methods used in both the overstuffed chair and the wing chair. Compare the design features of your furniture item with those shown, and use the upholstery methods that suit your particular project.

Getting STARTED

Tools

Quality upholstery cannot be achieved without the use of a few specially designed tools. If you make the initial investment in these tools and learn the proper way to use them, upholstery projects will be easier to complete and produce more satisfactory results. Tools can be purchased at upholstery supply stores or through catalogs or websites. Check the Yellow Pages or the Internet for the nearest supplier.

STRIPPING & UPHOLSTERING TOOLS

Claw-shaped tack and staple removers (1) are designed for removing old tacks and staples when stripping furniture to be reupholstered. A small screwdriver (2) can also be used to remove old tacks or staples. An upholsterer's tack hammer (3) has one magnetized tip, so that the hammer holds the tack, leaving your other hand free to hold the fabric. The style shown has a nylon tip, used for inserting decorative tacks. An electric staple gun (4) is a fast, efficient way to secure new fabric. Purchase a style that will accommodate both 3/8" (1 cm) and 1/2" (1.3 cm) staples. Replacing worn or loose webbing is a chore made infinitely easier by using a webbing stretcher (5). It works as a lever, allowing you to pull the webbing taut with one hand while tacking or stapling it with the other hand. Mallets (6), made of rubber or rawhide, are used to close flexible metal tack strips and to adjust padded surfaces. Stretching pliers (7), made for webbing and leather, can also be used to grasp and stretch fabric for stapling to the frame. Upholstery regulators (8), available in 8" (20.3 cm) and 10" (25.4 cm) lengths, are long metal skewers with multiple uses. The flattened end of the regulator is used for pleating or forcing padding into tight corners. The sharp end of the regulator is used to make a hole in the fabric by gently separating yarns in the weave. Once the padding has been moved, the hole can be closed by gently coaxing the yarns back into position.

MEASURING, MARKING & CUTTING TOOLS

Frequently, during the upholstery process, a yardstick (meterstick) (9) is necessary. Since most upholstery is not flat, you will also need a good-quality cloth tape measure (10). Dustless white chalk sticks (11) are used for marking out cutting lines on the fabric, for tailoring cushion patterns, and for various other marking tasks. A cutting mat and rotary cutter (12) make short work of cutting fabric strips for welting. Also be sure to have heavy-duty shears (13) for cutting the upholstery fabrics, battings, and other supplies.

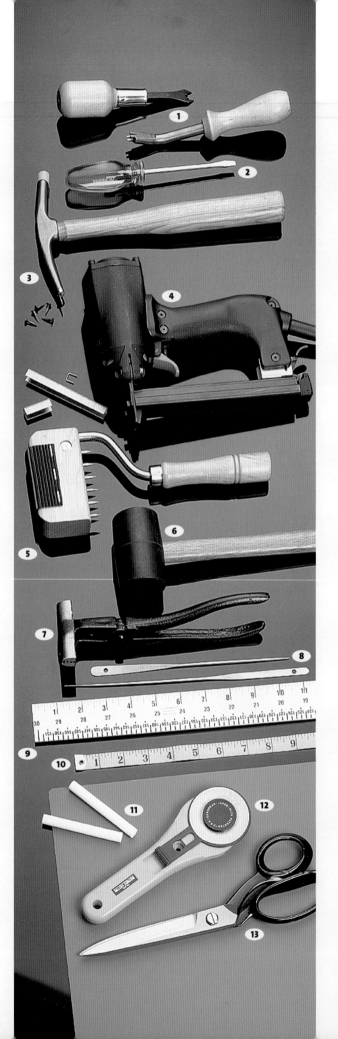

PINS & NEEDLES

There are several hand-sewing needles designed for upholstery work. Curved needles (1) are used for blind-stitching fabric in places where stapling or tacking are not possible. They are also used to secure springs to webbing and burlap. Round-point curved needles are used for fabrics, while wedge-point needles are used for leather or vinyl. Button needles (2), available in a variety of lengths from 6" to 18" (15.2 to 45.7 cm), are used to secure buttons to upholstered furniture and to stitch through padding to secure it to a foundation. Upholstery pins (3) are used to hold fabric in place temporarily before tacking or sewing.

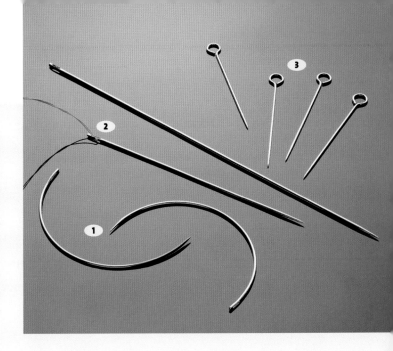

SEWING MACHINE EQUIPMENT

Though professional upholsterers use industrial sewing machines, most home sewing machines can successfully handle lightweight to medium-weight upholstery fabrics. Some specially designed accessories can help to make the job easier.

Insert heavy-duty needles into the sewing machine. For lightweight to medium-weight upholstery fabrics, use size 16/100 (1); for heavyweight fabrics, use size 18/110 (2). Specially designed needles for sewing on leathers and vinyls (3) have a wedge-shaped point that cuts a tiny slit, rather than a round hole.

A welting foot is very helpful for sewing continuous welting without puckers. A deep groove cut in the bottom of the foot rides over the fabric-covered cord, feeding the layers of fabric evenly for a smooth, tight fit. If a welting foot is not available for your sewing machine brand, you may be able to use a generic foot, such as the Pearls 'N Piping Foot (4) made by Creative Feet, which is designed to accommodate welting and trim up to $1/4$" (6 mm) thick. A zipper foot (5) is essential for inserting zippers into cushions and can also be used for making welting, if a welting foot is not available. A general-purpose foot (6) or a straight-stitch foot (7) can be used for sewing any seam that does not have welting. A walking foot (8) can be used to keep layers from shifting when sewing unwelted seams in difficult fabrics, such as upholstery velvet.

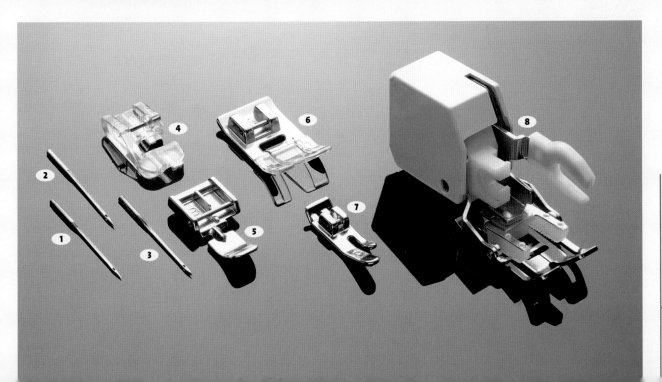

Upholstery Supplies

The basic shape and foundation padding in any piece of furniture is formed using a variety of materials. Many modern pieces use synthetic foam to provide the basic shaping and are padded with polyester batting. Others, especially older pieces, are shaped and padded using natural-fiber foundation materials, such as rubberized hair or coirtex, which is no longer available, and then padded with cotton batting. Often, furniture contains both natural and synthetic foundation materials, as when an overstuffed chair has natural-fiber padding in the arms and back, and a foam seat cushion wrapped with polyester batting.

When reupholstering a piece of furniture that was originally padded with natural-fiber materials, reuse the materials intact, if the foundation is still in very good shape. Supplement or replace the padding with either cotton or polyester batting. If the original foundation materials are not reusable, build a new foundation using foam and polyester batting, which are more readily available, more economical, and easier to work with.

To retain authenticity, reupholster antiques using natural materials. In stripping older furniture, it is common to discover padding materials such as curled hair, moss, tow, and straw. If desired, these materials can be reused, though it may be impossible to supplement the padding with more of the same material, and working with these materials requires more time and expertise. Often some additional cotton batting is all that is needed to restore the piece to its original shape and firmness.

PADDING MATERIALS

Foam (1) can be purchased in many thicknesses and degrees of firmness. High-resilience foams are used for seat cushions because of their superior ability to retain their shape. Upholsterers cut foam with an electric foam saw that features a vertical blade. An electric kitchen knife can also be used, but care must be taken to keep the blade perpendicular to the surface of the foam for perfectly squared cuts. Foam that is 1" (2.5 cm) thick or thinner can be cut with shears. Spray foam adhesive (2) is used to secure foam to webbing or polyester batting.

Bonded polyester batting (3), noted for its loft and resiliency, is commonly used in most modern upholstered furniture. Polyester batting is cut with shears. It can be stapled directly to framework and need not be covered by an inner cover.

Cotton batting (4) is available in different grades of purity, depending on the intended use. Economy grades of cotton tend to be less fluffy and may contain seeds and other impurities. For surface padding, a high grade of cotton is used. Cotton batting is gently torn to size, rather than cut.

Deck pad (5) is a stiff padding material made from polyester fibers that are thermally bonded and needled for strength. Because it is rather thin, deck pad is suitable for areas that require minimal foundation padding, such as chair decks or thinly padded chair backs or arms.

Rubberized hair (6) is used when a thicker or fuller appearance is required. Some types make a crunching sound when they are compressed, but this can be minimized by layering it with cotton batting.

6

5

4

3

FOUNDATION FABRICS

Cambric (1) is a black fabric used to cover the bottom of a furniture piece for a finished look and to act as a dustcover.

Burlap (2) is used as a covering over springs or webbing to form the support base.

Denim (3) is a strong, thin fabric, available in many colors to coordinate with upholstery fabric. It is used to cover the deck area of the chair and to line skirts. Webbing, purchased in rolls, is available in both synthetic (4) and jute (5) forms. Synthetic webbing is stronger than true jute webbing and does not rot over time or due to moisture. Jute webbing, however, is necessary for reupholstering antiques to retain their authenticity.

An edge roll (6) is a long, firmly stuffed tube that is attached over a wood or wire edge to cushion it. Edge rolls, available in a variety of sizes, keep padding from shifting, while reducing wear on the other fabric.

THREADS, TWINES & CORDS

Polyester thread (7) is the best choice for upholstery sewing using a conventional sewing machine. It offers strength, without being too thick. Nylon thread, size #18 (8), works well for any hand sewing that must be done, because it fits the eyes of curved needles and is available in many colors. Nylon button twine (9) is a strong twine used for various tasks, such as fastening buttons, hand-stitching edge rolls and nosing seams, and securing springs to webbing and burlap. Spring twine (10), available in both jute and polyester, is used for tying springs (page 32). Welt cording (11) is most commonly used in the $^5/_{32}$" (3.8 mm) size. Cotton cording provides the best results for most upholstery fabrics.

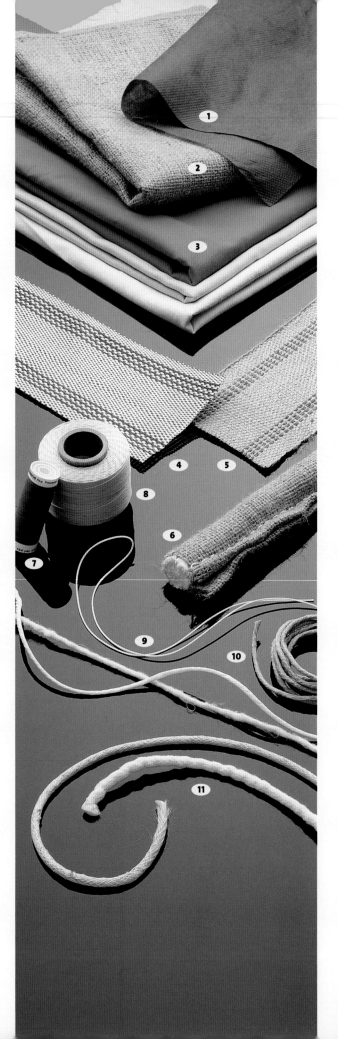

NAILS, TACKS, STAPLES & ZIPPERS

Webbing nails (1), as the name implies, are used to secure webbing to the frame. Because they are narrow and have sharp points, they can hold the webbing securely without damaging the wood. They are also used to secure the tails of hand-sewing threads, and in other cases where upholstery tacks are not sufficient. The most commonly used sizes of upholstery tacks (2) are #3 and #6, the smaller number relating to the shorter tacks. Upholstery tacks are packaged in sterile condition, recognizing that the most convenient place to hold them is in the mouth. Staples (3) are the fastener of choice for most upholstery tasks, except reupholstering antique furniture, in which case, tacks are used. Decorative tacks (4) come in many sizes, designs, and finishes to complement any fabric or furniture style. Tack strip (5) is cardboard stripping, 1/2" (1.3 cm) wide, used to maintain a straight, sharp line between upholstered fabric pieces. Tacking strip (6) has tacks spaced evenly apart for securing fabric panels invisibly, when tacking is not possible. Flexible metal tacking strip (7) is used for the same purpose in curved areas.

Strong zippers, available with either metal or nylon teeth, are used for cushion cover closures. They can be purchased in predetermined lengths (8) or as continuous zipper tape (9), which can be cut to size and fitted with a zipper pull.

Upholstery Fabrics

The fabric selected for the upholstery project has a great impact on the final appearance, comfort, and durability of the furniture piece. Color and design obviously play a large part in the decision making, but it is also important to consider the fiber content, weave structure, and any surface treatment applied to the fabric.

Various fibers are used in upholstery fabrics, including natural and synthetic types. Some natural fibers come from a plant source, such as cotton, linen, or ramie. Others are animal products, such as wool or silk. Synthetic fibers include nylon, acrylic, polyester, and olefin. Rayon is a man-made fiber, produced from a plant source.

Each fiber has characteristics that make it desirable in some ways, though limiting its appeal in other ways. Often fibers are blended in a fabric to capitalize on the strengths of each, while minimizing their weaknesses. Rayon, for example, does not wear well but is often blended with fibers that are stronger because it accepts dye well and gives the fabric luster. Natural fibers are generally easier to work with than synthetics. However, synthetics blended with natural fibers often produce a more stable fabric.

Some fabrics are woven so the pattern or design is *railroaded*. This means running the lengthwise grain horizontally on the piece of furniture rather than in the normal vertical direction. Railroading can save a considerable amount of fabric, especially on sofas.

Fabrics can be grouped into categories according to their weave or surface design. Plain weaves (1) are the simplest of weaves. Their durability depends on the strength of the yarns and closeness of the weave. Satin weaves (2) are woven so that yarns float on the surface, giving the fabric a subtle sheen. They are often printed and can be used for drapery or upholstery. Rib weaves (3) are a variation of the plain weave. Finer yarns alternate with heavier yarns, giving the ribbed effect. Their durability is limited because the yarns are exposed to friction during use. Pile weaves (4) have cut or uncut loops that stand up on the surface of the fabric. Velvets and chenilles are pile weaves. Jacquard weaves (5) have a woven-in design, created on a special loom. Damasks, tapestries, and brocades are all jacquard weaves. Novelty weaves (6) are created by using a variation or a combination of the basic weaves.

Most upholstery fabrics are treated with a stain-resistant or crease-resistant finish, greatly increasing the durability of the fabric. A latex finish is sometimes applied to the back of loosely woven or pile fabrics to keep the grain line from shifting or to hold the pile in place. A heavy latex backing makes the fabric quite stiff and difficult to sew.

Furniture Parts

Learning the process and techniques of furniture upholstery will be eased by knowing the correct names of the furniture parts, both in their upholstered state and stripped to the bare frame. Use the labeled photographs below and opposite to become familiar with these part names. Depending on the project, the furniture piece you are upholstering may not have all the parts that are shown on the chair below. Or it may have parts not shown, such as a skirt, arm boxing, or back boxing.

UPHOLSTERED PARTS

(1) INSIDE BACK

(2) INSIDE WING

(3) OUTSIDE BACK

(4) OUTSIDE WING

(5) INSIDE ARM

(6) FRONT ARM BAND

(7) ARM PANEL

(8) OUTSIDE ARM

(9) WELTING

(10) CUSHION

(11) CUSHION BOXING

(12) DECK
(UNDER CUSHION)

(13) NOSING

(14) FRONT BAND

FRAME PARTS

(1) TOP BACK RAIL

(2) TOP WING RAIL

(3) FRONT WING POST

(4) TOP ARM RAIL

(5) FRONT ARM POST

(6) ARM STRETCHER RAIL

(7) FRONT RAIL

(8) CORNER BLOCK

(9) BACK RAIL

(10) BACK STRETCHER RAIL

(11) BACK STRETCHER POST

(12) SIDE RAIL

(13) BACK LEG POST

MEASURE AND RECORD THE ACTUAL SIZE OF EACH SECTION, INCLUDING THE APPROXIMATE AMOUNT OF HIDDEN FABRIC. DETERMINE THE CUT SIZE OF EACH SECTION BY ADDING THE NECESSARY ALLOWANCES FOR PULLING AND STAPLING OR FOR SEAMS, AS EXPLAINED AT RIGHT. DOUBLE-CHECK YOUR LIST TO BE SURE THAT YOU HAVE NOT FORGOTTEN ANY SECTIONS. THEN DIAGRAM THE FABRIC LAYOUT FROM THE DETERMINED CUT SIZES.

Measuring & Cutting

Before stripping the cover from the furniture, take careful measurements of every piece. This is important not only for determining fabric requirements but also for planning an efficient cutting layout. Keep in mind that most pieces will be cut out as rectangles and trimmed to shape as they are attached to the furniture. It is important, therefore, to measure each piece at its longest and widest points.

Make a list of all the pieces that will be needed, and record the measurements as they are taken. Write the measurements as length times width, remembering that length is always the up-and-down measurement; width is always the side-to-side measurement. Then add in the necessary allowances, adding a 2" (5.1 cm) pulling allowance to each edge that will be attached by stapling or tacking and 1/2" (1.3 cm) seam allowances to pieces that are sewn together. Finally, measure the total length of all the welting used in the furniture piece. The example chart below was developed from the measurements of the chair shown opposite. Your measurement chart may include pieces not listed on the example chart, such as a skirt, arm boxing, or back boxing.

The total length of some pieces, including inside back, inside arms, and inside wings, includes fabric that cannot be seen before stripping. From the point where the inside back meets the deck, for example, hidden fabric extends down several inches (centimeters) and is attached to the back rail of the chair. Include the approximate amount of hidden fabric in your actual measurements.

To avoid wasting expensive upholstery fabric, strips of inexpensive fabrics or used upholstery fabrics, called stretchers, are often sewn to the pieces in hidden locations. To determine the cut size of a piece that will get a stretcher, measure the visible fabric and add 1/2" (1.3 cm) for each edge that is attached to another piece by a seam and 2" (5.1 cm) to each edge that will have a stretcher. This will ensure that the stretcher is not visible in the finished upholstery. Cut the stretcher to the size of the hidden fabric plus 2" (5.1 cm).

After measuring, diagram the layout of all the pieces on graph paper, as in the examples on pages 22 and 23. The amount of fabric needed can be accurately determined from the diagram. To avoid costly mistakes, purchase fabric only after completing the measuring and layout diagram.

Cut the end of the fabric squarely, either by following a thread in the weave, using a carpenter's square, or aligning a straightedge to the pattern repeat markings on the selvages. Transfer the diagram to the right side of the fabric, marking out the cutting lines with chalk and measuring from the squared end. Label the wrong side of every piece with its location as it is cut. Also, draw a chalk line near the lower edge to indicate the downward direction.

MEASUREMENT CHART EXAMPLE

PIECE	ACTUAL SIZE (includes hidden fabric)		ALLOWANCES 1/2" (1.3 cm) seam 2" (5.1 cm) pulling		CUT SIZE
FRONT BAND (FB)	5 1/2" x 21" (14 x 53.3 CM)	+	2 1/2" x 4" (6.4 x 10.2 CM)	=	8" x 25" (20.3 x 63.5 CM)
NOSING (N)	6" x 21" (15.2 x 53.3 CM)	+	1" x 4" (2.5 x 10.2 CM)	=	7" x 25" (17.8 x 63.5 CM)
INSIDE BACK (IB)	36" x 32" (91.4 x 81.3 CM)	+	4" x 4" (10.2 x 10.2 CM)	=	40" x 36" (101.6 x 91.4 CM)
INSIDE ARM (IA)	27" x 27" (68.6 x 68.6 CM)	+	4" x 4" (10.2 x 10.2 CM)	=	31" x 31" (78.7 x 78.7 CM)
FRONT ARM BAND (FAB)	18" x 8" (45.7 x 20.3 CM)	+	4" x 2 1/2" (10.2 x 6.4 CM)	=	22" x 10 1/2" (55.9 x 26.9 CM)
INSIDE WING (IW)	17" x 9" (43.2 x 22.9 CM)	+	4" x 4" (10.2 x 10.2 CM)	=	21" x 13" (53.3 x 33 CM)
OUTSIDE ARM (OA)	14" x 26" (35.6 x 66 CM)	+	4" x 4" (10.2 x 10.2 CM)	=	18" x 30" (45.7 x 76.2 CM)
OUTSIDE WING (OW)	15" x 7" (38.1 x 17.8 CM)	+	4" x 4" (10.2 x 10.2 CM)	=	19" x 11" (48.3 x 27.9 CM)
OUTSIDE BACK (OB)	30" x 23" (76.2 x 58.4 CM)	+	4" x 4" (10.2 x 10.2 CM)	=	34" x 27" (86.4 x 68.6 CM)
ARM PANEL (AP)	15 1/2" x 4" (39.4 x 10.2 CM)	+	4" x 4" (10.2 x 10.2 CM)	=	19 1/2" x 8" (49.5 x 20.3 CM)
CUSHION* (C)	22" x 19" (55.9 x 48.3 CM)				
CUSHION BOXING* (CB)	4" x 63" (10.2 x 160 CM)				
ZIPPER BOXING* (ZB)	2" x 26" (5.1 x 66 CM)				
WELTING** (W)	250" (635 CM)				266" x 1 5/8" (676 x 4.1 CM)

*The cut size of cushion pieces, cushion boxing, and zipper boxing are determined after tailoring a pattern for the cushion (page 50).
**Additional welting length is allowed for seaming and waste.

FABRIC LAYOUT DIAGRAMS

Layout for Fabric without a Pattern.

1. Most upholstery fabrics are 54" (137 cm) wide. Because the pieces are cut as rectangles, this layout is suitable for fabric with or without a nap.

Layout for Railroaded Fabric.

2. If the fabric can be railroaded (page 17), lay out the pieces so that their length runs on the crosswise grain. This is often a more efficient layout.

Layout for Patterned Fabric.

3. Special consideration must be given to the length of the repeat and the pattern arrangement. Large motifs, indicated by dots on the diagram, are centered on the exposed areas of prominent pieces, such as cushion tops and bottoms, inside and outside backs, and inside and outside arms. The pattern should flow uninterrupted from the top of the inside back to the bottom of the front band or skirt, aligning horizontally, as well.

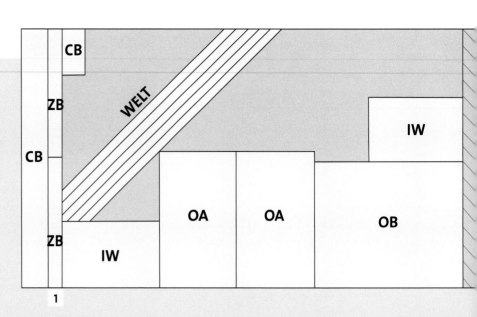

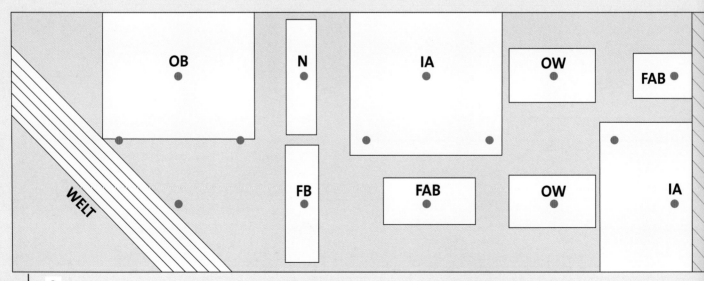

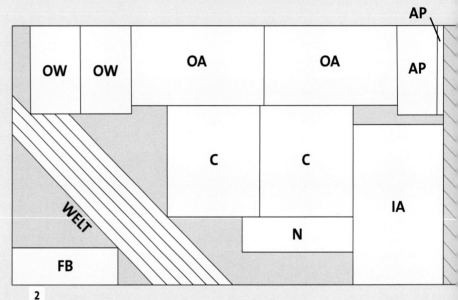

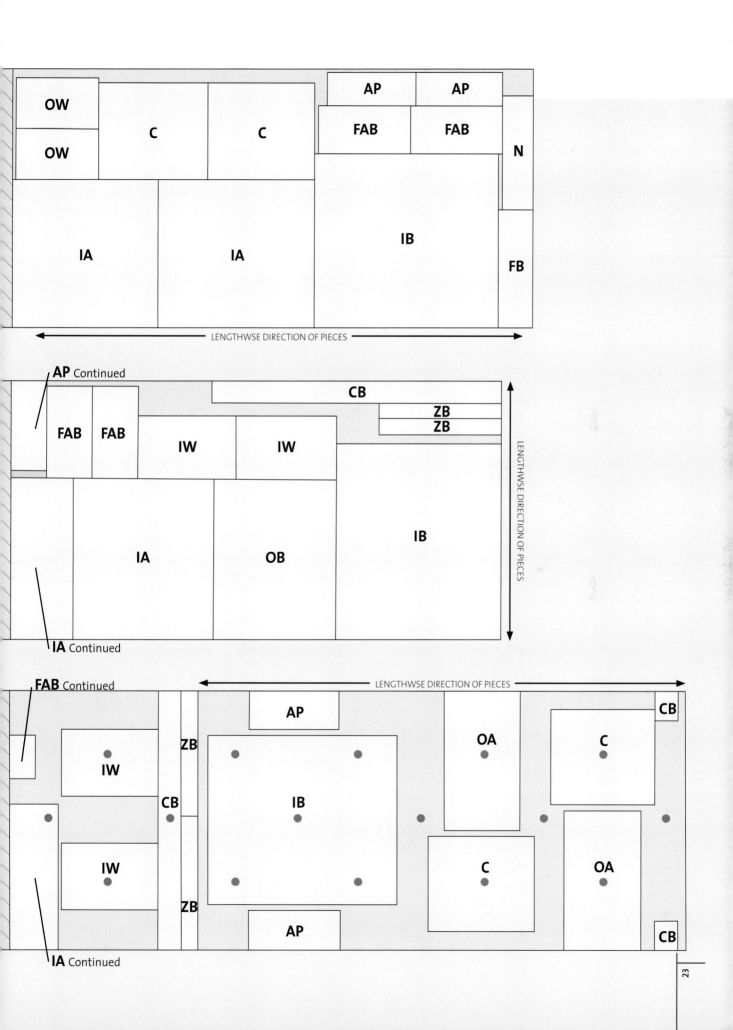

OW

OW

C

C

AP

AP

FAB

FAB

N

IA

IA

IB

FB

LENGTHWSE DIRECTION OF PIECES

AP Continued

FAB

FAB

IW

IW

CB

ZB

ZB

IA

OB

IB

IA Continued

LENGTHWSE DIRECTION OF PIECES

FAB Continued

LENGTHWSE DIRECTION OF PIECES

CB

IW

ZB

AP

OA

C

CB

IB

C

IW

ZB

AP

C

OA

CB

IA Continued

COVER YOUR WORK AREA WITH A TARP. STRIPPING UPHOLSTERY IS MESSY AND DUSTY. DISCARD USED TACKS, NAILS, STAPLES, TACK STRIPS, AND TACKING STRIPS; THEY ARE NOT REUSABLE. DISCARD ANY MUSTY-SMELLING FOUNDATION MATERIALS. TAKE DETAILED NOTES, AND DRAW SKETCHES OR TAKE PICTURES WITH EVERY PIECE THAT IS REMOVED. THESE WILL BECOME YOUR REUPHOLSTERY INSTRUCTIONS.

Stripping Furniture

Removing the old cover from a furniture piece is an educational experience, so take notes. Before removing even one staple, sketch or take pictures of any unique details you wish to reproduce in the new cover, such as the pleating arrangement on an arm front or a series of tucks at a nosing corner. Determine any areas that need more padding. Label each fabric piece with its location and direction. List the seams and joints that have welting, and measure the total length of welting used. Once removed, the fabric pieces are merely puzzling flat shapes.

Avoid back strain and sore knees by standing the project on a raised platform or padded sawhorses. You can then do the upholstery work while standing or sitting at a comfortable height, without repeatedly bending over or kneeling.

Loosen or remove pieces in the reverse order from that in which they were attached to the frame. For example, in reupholstering a wing chair, first remove the skirt, dustcover, and any welting around the lower edge. Then remove the outside back, outside arms, and outside wings. Loosen the inside back, inside arms, and inside wings, leaving them staple-basted (page 68) in position to keep the padding in place. Remove the deck and nosing last. As each piece is loosened or removed, record the method used to attach it to adjoining pieces or to the frame: machine-sewn, hand-sewn, stapled, or attached with a tacking strip. Set the pieces aside for reference throughout the upholstery project.

Strip the padding and foundation only as far as necessary. Check to see if the frame is sturdy, if the webbing and springs are secure, and if the padding needs to be replaced or replenished. Some furniture will have a muslin cover just under the outer cover. This can be left intact if only the outer cover needs to be replaced. However, if you encounter any additional layers of old upholstery fabric, remove them.

TIPS FOR STRIPPING UPHOLSTERY

Removing tacks, nails, and staples
1. HOLD the tack lifter or staple remover at a sharp angle, with the tip touching the wood at the edge of the tack, nail, or staple. Strike the end of the handle with the side of the tack hammer, wedging the tip under the tack, nail, or staple.

2. PRY the tack, nail, or staple up from the wood.

3. GRASP the tack, nail, or staple with the pliers; roll the pliers in the direction of the wood grain, extracting the tack, nail, or staple. (Extracting against the wood grain damages and weakens the wood.) Remove all tacks, nails, and staples. Pound in any broken points that cannot be removed.

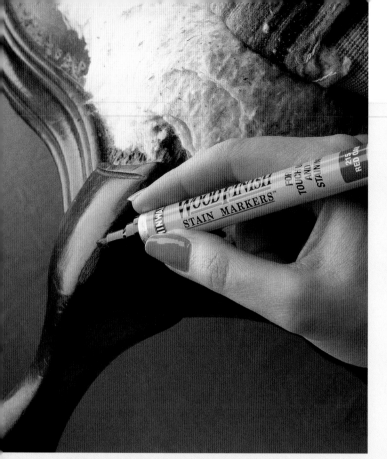

Easy Frame Repairs

Because you are about to spend considerable time, energy, and money on reupholstering, it is important to begin with a structurally sound furniture frame. After removing the outer cover, check to see if there are any loose joints or cracked rails or posts. Minor repair work can be done with minimal carpentry skills.

This is also the opportune time to completely refinish any exposed wood, if necessary. However, shallow scratches and general dullness can be corrected with simpler techniques.

REPAIR minor scratches, using touch-up markers in the same color as the stained and finished woodwork.

CLEAN a dull finish, using wood polish and cleaner and gently rubbing with extra-fine steel wool. Cleaners containing lemon oil are especially beneficial.

TIGHTEN loose corner blocks by first applying wood glue and then inserting wood screws.

To reglue loose joints

1. OPEN the joint. Apply hot vinegar to the old glue to soften; scrape away the old glue.

2. APPLY an ample amount of wood glue to the joint. Close the joint; clamp tightly. Allow to dry, following the glue manufacturer's directions.

Cracked rail or post

1. INJECT wood glue into the crack, using a glue syringe.

2. CLAMP the rail or post securely. Allow to dry, following the glue manufacturer's directions.

Webbing

The support base for most furniture consists of interwoven strips of webbing. Webbing is used in seats, backs, and arms as a base for springs or padding, and ultimately takes the weight of the person sitting or leaning on it. Whenever reupholstering a piece of furniture, check the existing webbing for wear and tautness. Unless the furniture is fairly new, it is probably worth the time and effort to replace the webbing with new taut strips.

Webbing is usually 3½" (8.9 cm) wide and available in several strengths. Synthetic webbing and webbing made from a blend of jute and synthetic fibers, such as Jutelac, are very stable and can be used in all locations. Jute webbing with a red stripe is designed to be used in seats, because it will not stretch. Jute webbing with a black stripe is slightly less stable and is used for the arms and backs of chairs and sofas. A webbing stretcher (page 10) makes the job much easier and is essential for attaching the strips with the proper tautness. For efficiency and easy handling, work from the roll of webbing; do not precut webbing strips. Webbing nails must be used for securing seat and back webbing. Webbing on parts that do not bear much weight may be secured with staples, if desired.

Generally, a seat with springs is webbed on the underside of the frame; a seat without springs is webbed on the upper side of the frame. Arms, backs, and wings without springs are webbed on the inner surfaces; backs or arms with springs are webbed on the outer surfaces. The more weight the webbing must hold, the closer together the strips should be, always allowing at least ¼" (6 mm) between them to prevent abrasion. Webbing on arms or wings that will not bear weight can be spaced up to 4" (10.2 cm) apart.

You Will Need

- Webbing
- Webbing nails
- Webbing stretcher
- #6 upholstery tacks; tack hammer

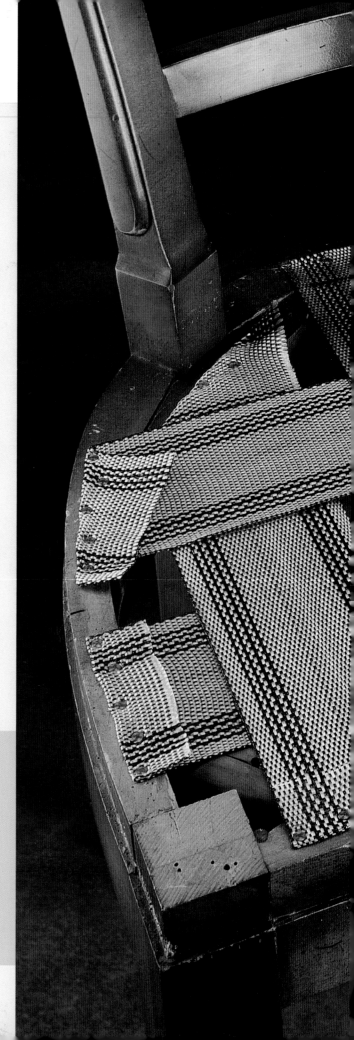

SYNTHETIC WEBBING, PULLED TAUT AND PROPERLY SECURED, PROVIDES A FIRM, LONG-LASTING SUPPORT BASE.

HOW TO ATTACH WEBBING TO A SEAT

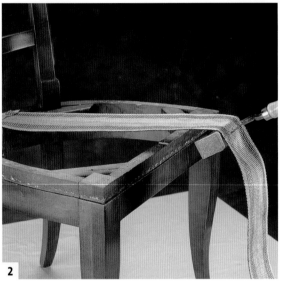

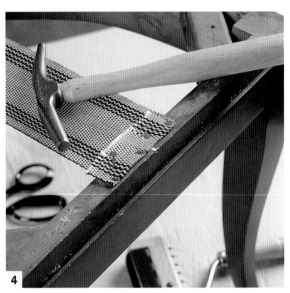

1. MARK the centers of the front and back rails. Determine the number and spacing of the strips. Fold back the webbing 1" (2.5 cm). Place the folded end ¼" (6 mm) from the outer edge of the back rail, centering the strip over the center mark if using an odd number of strips or placing a strip to one side of the center mark if using an even number. Secure the folded end to the rail, using five webbing nails arranged as shown (nail heads painted for visibility).

2. DRAW the webbing across the frame opening to the front rail, centering the strip over the center front mark or to one side of the center. Place the webbing stretcher under the webbing, catching the webbing securely on the stretcher spikes.

3. WEDGE the stretcher under the front rail. Pull the webbing taut, taking care not to bend the rails; insert three #6 tacks in the center of the rail to hold the webbing.

4. TRIM the webbing 1" (2.5 cm) beyond the outer edge of the rail. Fold back the end of the strip so the fold is ¼" (6 mm) from the outer edge of the rail. Insert five webbing nails, positioned as shown.

5. ATTACH the remaining webbing strips from the back to the front, evenly spaced; alternate them from side to side of the center. Stretch all the strips equally taut.

6. MARK the centers of the side rails. Attach the first webbing strip in a sideways direction, at or to one side of the center; weave the strip over and under previously attached strips. Attach the remaining strips, alternating from side to side of the center and reversing the weave pattern of adjacent strips.

Back webbing (top)
Attach the vertical webbing strips first, stretching them from bottom to top. Weave and secure the horizontal strips, starting near the center of the back.

Arm or wing webbing (bottom)
Space the webbing strips up to 4" (10.2 cm) apart, providing minimal foundation for the padding. For a chair without an arm stretcher post, pin back the end of the front-to-back strip until the inside back and inside arm cover pieces have been attached.

Springs

The basic shape and resilience of upholstered furniture is achieved with the use of steel springs. Depending on the style and age of the furniture, it may contain either *coil springs* or *sinuous springs*.

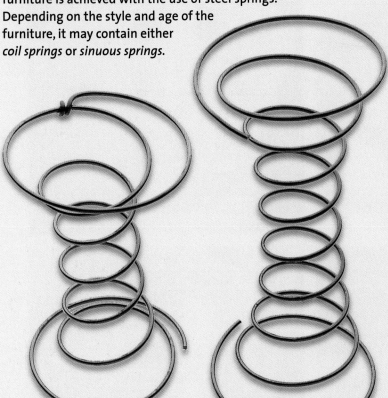

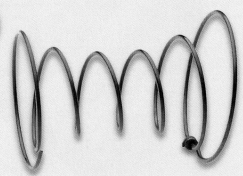

COIL SPRINGS ARE MANUFACTURED IN VARIOUS STYLES, SIZES, AND GAUGES, AND THREE DEGREES OF FIRMNESS: HARD, MEDIUM, AND SOFT. THE TOP AND BOTTOM COILS MAY BE OPEN WITH THE ENDS BENT SLIGHTLY INWARD, OR THE TOP COIL MAY BE CLOSED. IN TYPICAL HOURGLASS-SHAPED SPRINGS, FIRMNESS IS DETERMINED BY THE TIGHTNESS OF THE CENTER COILS. ALWAYS REPLACE BROKEN OR BENT SPRINGS WITH MATCHING ONES.

Coil springs are commonly found in seats and may also provide shape in arms and backs. Several coil springs, arranged in rows, are individually sewn to webbing and then systematically tied together, so that they work as a unit. In some furniture, the coil springs are attached to metal crossbars, rather than webbing, and replacement parts may be difficult to find. The entire system can be rebuilt with a webbing base, if necessary. Often, the coil springs are tied or clipped to an edge wire, secured around all or part of the outer edge. This is used for a flat surface, such as the deck of an overstuffed chair. Spring systems for dome-shaped seats, backs, or ottomans are tied without edge wires.

Some modern furniture is constructed with sinuous springs: heavy steel wire shaped in repeating S-curves. These are attached with metal clips to the furniture frame and then tied together with spring twine to prevent them from tipping sideways. In stripping a piece of furniture with sinuous springs, you may find that they are linked to each other by small helical springs or metal straps, rather than spring twine.

Before reupholstering a piece of furniture, you should check the condition of the spring system. If it is intact and sturdy, the piece can be reupholstered as it is. Any broken or bent springs must be replaced, using a spring of the same gauge, size, and degree of firmness. To be assured of buying the correct spring, compare it to one from the system that is still in good condition. It is a good idea to retie the entire spring system if any of the twines have loosened or broken, or if the webbing supporting the springs needs to be replaced.

In the spring-tying methods described on pages 34 to 43, the springs in each row are lashed together with the first twine, making simple loops over the coils. This enables you to set the height of the springs and adjust their positions before permanently tying them with the second twine. Tying springs may seem complicated, but if you follow this method and use the recommended knots, the system will remain secure and well shaped for many years.

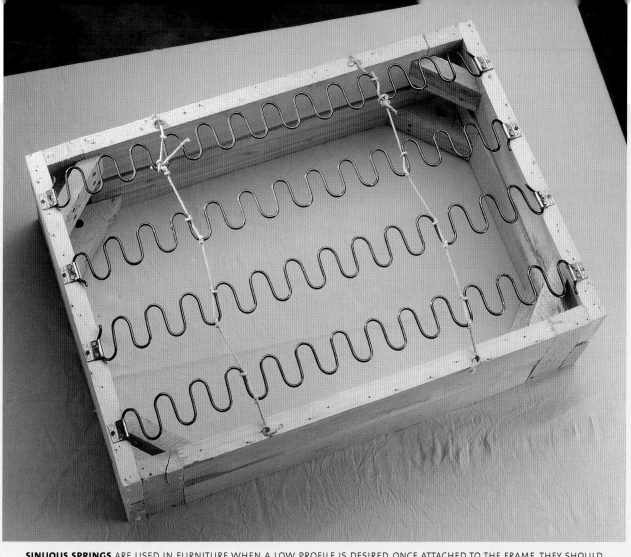

SINUOUS SPRINGS ARE USED IN FURNITURE WHEN A LOW PROFILE IS DESIRED. ONCE ATTACHED TO THE FRAME, THEY SHOULD RISE IN A SLIGHT ARC, NO MORE THAN 1¹/2" (3.8 CM) HIGH. BECAUSE THEY ARE VERY DURABLE, SINUOUS SPRINGS RARELY NEED TO BE REPLACED BUT MAY NEED TO BE RETIED, USING CLOVE HITCH KNOTS OR OVERHAND KNOTS.

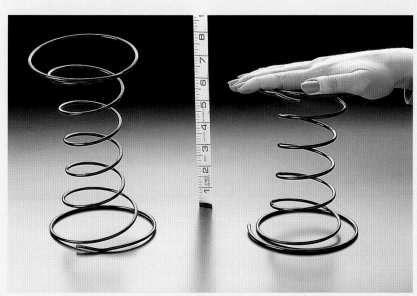

COMPRESS THE COIL SPRING UNTIL IT RESISTS COMPRESSION, TO DETERMINE THE HEIGHT AT WHICH IT SHOULD BE TIED. SEAT SPRINGS ARE TYPICALLY COMPRESSED 1¹/2" (3.8 CM) BELOW THEIR ACTUAL HEIGHT.

You Will Need

Coil spring system

- Coil springs
- 6" (15.2 cm) curved needle and nylon button twine
- Spring twine
- Webbing nails
- Ruler
- Edge wire, for edge wire system

Sinuous spring system

- Sinuous springs, clips, and nails
- Spring twine

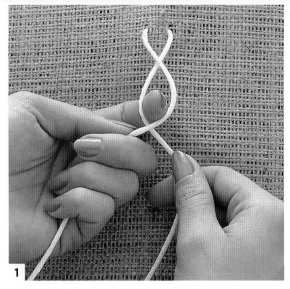

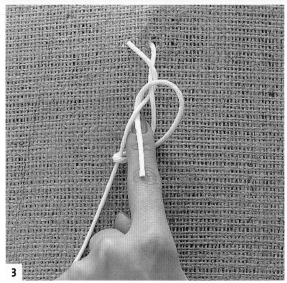

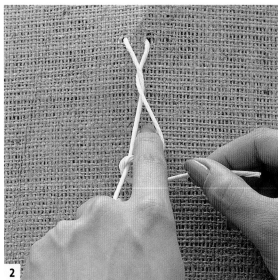

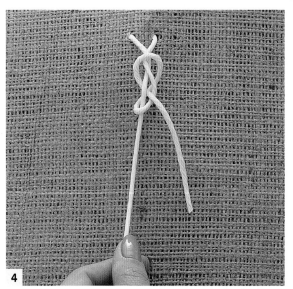

Slipknot

1. TAKE one stitch, leaving a tail. Hold the long end of the twine in the left hand, the tail in the right hand. Hook the tail with the index finger of the left hand, pulling the tail behind the other twine.

2. TURN the left hand over, twisting the twines.

3. WRAP the tail over the twisted twines above the index finger, wrapping to the back of the twist; insert the tail end in the first loop above the finger.

4. REMOVE the index finger; pull on the long end of the twine to tighten.

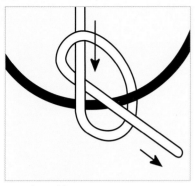

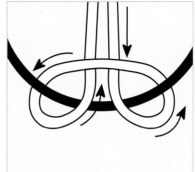

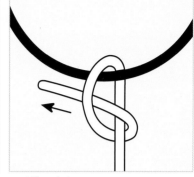

Overhand knot　　　*Clove hitch knot*　　　*Half hitch knot*

HOW TO SEW COIL SPRINGS TO WEBBING

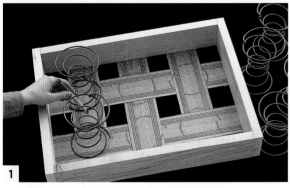

1

3

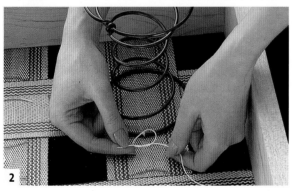

2

4

1. ARRANGE the springs over the webbing in desired row formation, placing the springs over the webbing intersections, 2" to 4" (5.1 to 10.2 cm) apart; follow the original arrangement, if possible. Mark the locations with chalk. (A marker was used here for visibility.) If using open-ended springs, position them so the top open ends of the springs in the back row face forward; the remaining open ends face backward.

2. THREAD the 6" (15.2 cm) curved needle with nylon button twine. Beginning with a corner spring, insert the needle from the top of the webbing, next to the bottom coil. Take one short stitch, coming back through the webbing close to the opposite side of the coil; leave the tail for knotting. Secure the stitch with a slipknot. Tie an overhand knot over the slipknot.

3. INSERT the needle back through the webbing to the underside. Stitch the spring to the webbing with three more stitches, arranging the stitches so that the last stitch is located near the knot on the underside of the webbing.

4. SECURE each spring with four stitches, working one entire row; proceed to the next row. Plan the stitch placement so that the last stitch on each spring is near the first stitch on the next spring. Lock all the stitches between the first and the last stitch with overhand knots; lock the last stitch with a slipknot, followed by two overhand knots.

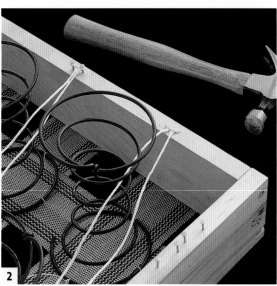

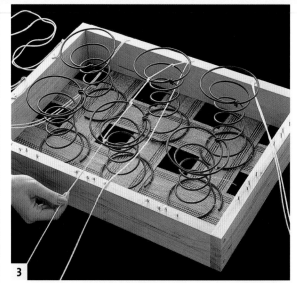

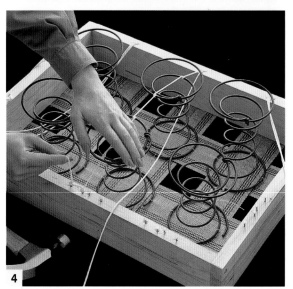

1. DRIVE two webbing nails, spaced ¹/₂" (1.3 cm) apart, halfway into the rail at the center of each row of springs on all rails. On the front rail and one side rail, drive two more nails halfway into the rail, each spaced 1" (2.5 cm) to the outside of the center nails.

2. CUT the spring twine for each row, with the length equal to four times the distance between the rails. Fold the twine in half. Slip the folded loop between the two nails on the back rail; wrap the loop back over the nails, as shown. Pull the twine snugly around the nails. Drive the nails tightly in the rail, securing the twine. Repeat for each set of nails on the back rail and on one side rail.

3. LASH the row of springs together, working them from back to front and starting with the row at or near the center. Follow the diagram (a), page 42; use single twine, wrapping over and around each spring coil in simple loops.

4. WRAP the twine once around one inner nail in the front rail; hold the twine taut with one hand while adjusting the height and position of the springs with the other hand. The springs should stand perpendicular to the webbing; the top coils of the front and back springs should angle slightly toward the rails. Wrap the twine around the outer nail; drive the nails tightly into the rail.

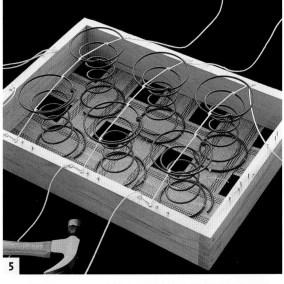

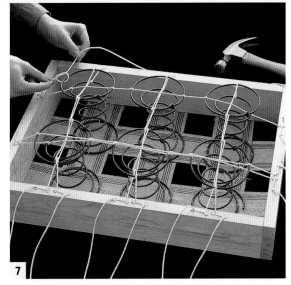

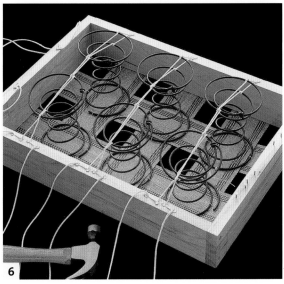

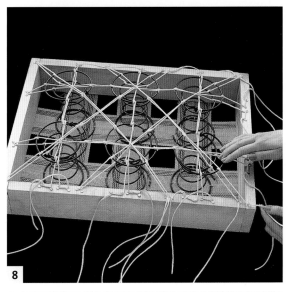

5. REPEAT steps 3 and 4 for all rows from back to front, checking the height and position of the springs frequently.

6. TIE the spring coils, using the remaining twine and following diagram (b), page 42. Use clove hitch knots or overhand knots at each location; tie knots over simple loops that share locations. Keep the twine tautness equal to the tautness of the first twine. Wrap twine around the remaining nails; drive nails tightly into the rail. Repeat for each back-to-front row.

7. TIE springs in side-to-side rows, following diagram (a) for the first twine and diagram (b) for the second twine; use clove hitch knots or overhand knots at each location for both twines, tying knots with equal tautness to previously tied twines.

8. LAY a straightedge across the center of the springs in a diagonal row; mark the rails at aligned points. Repeat for all diagonal rows. Drive two webbing nails, spaced 1/2" (1.3 cm) apart, halfway into the rail at each mark. Follow step 7 for each diagonal row. Cut tails to about 3" (7.6 cm).

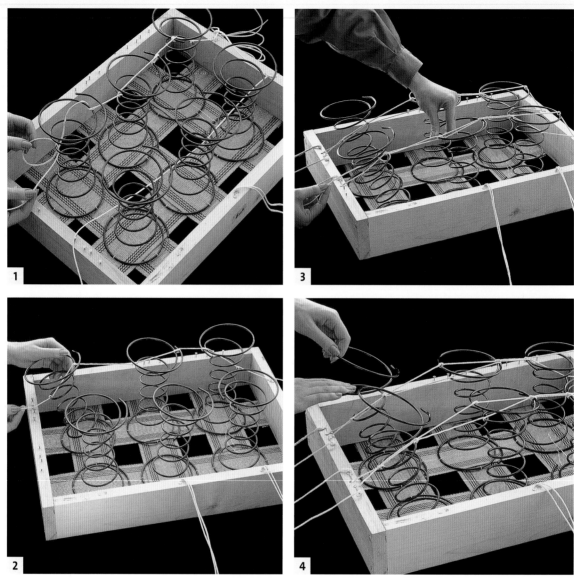

1. FOLLOW steps 1 and 2 on page 36, omitting nails and twine on the front side-to-side row and cutting twine for the back-to-front rows six times the distance between rails. Lash a row of springs together from back to front, using single twine; start with a row at or near the center. Follow diagram (c), page 42; wrap over and around each spring coil in simple loops.

2. WRAP twine once around one inner nail in the front rail; hold the twine taut with one hand while adjusting the height and position of springs with the other hand. All springs, except the front one, should stand perpendicular to the webbing. Pull the front spring forward until the front edge of the top coil is even with the front edge of the rail. Wrap twine around an outer nail; drive nails tightly into the rail.

3. LASH each back-to-front row, checking the height and position of the springs frequently. Tie spring coils, using the remaining twine and following diagram (d), page 43. Use clove hitch knots or overhand knots at each location; tie knots over simple loops that share locations. Keep the twine tautness equal to the tautness of the first twine. Wrap twine around the remaining nails; drive nails tightly into the rail.

4. FINISH tying all front-to-back rows. Spread the first and second coils of the front spring, increasing their resiliency. This is called "breaking" the springs.

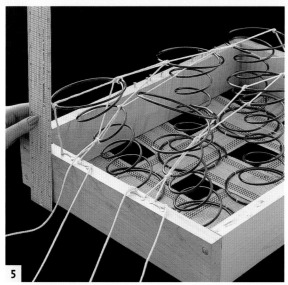

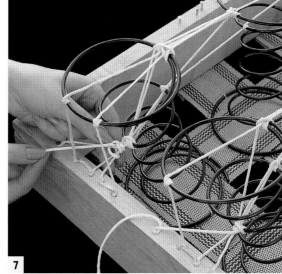

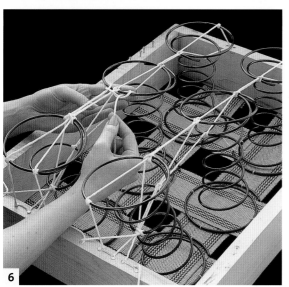

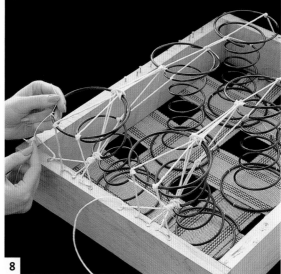

5. PULL one twine tail up to the top coil of the front spring; tie clove hitch knots around the front and then back of the top coil, tying the spring at the same height as the center springs. Continue tying clove hitch knots, following diagram (e), page 43. Secure twine to the rail, using another webbing nail. Repeat for each back-to-front row.

6. PULL the remaining twine tail up to the top coil of the front spring. Tie a clove hitch knot alongside the first knot. Then tie knots over the existing knots, following diagram (e), page 43.

7. TIE several half hitch knots around the twines between the third coil and the rail. Repeat for all back-to-front rows.

8. CUT a piece of button twine, about 70" (178 cm) long. Spread knots on the front top coil about 1¹/₂"(3.8 cm). Fold the twine in half; tie a clove hitch knot to the coil just outside one knot.

continued on next page

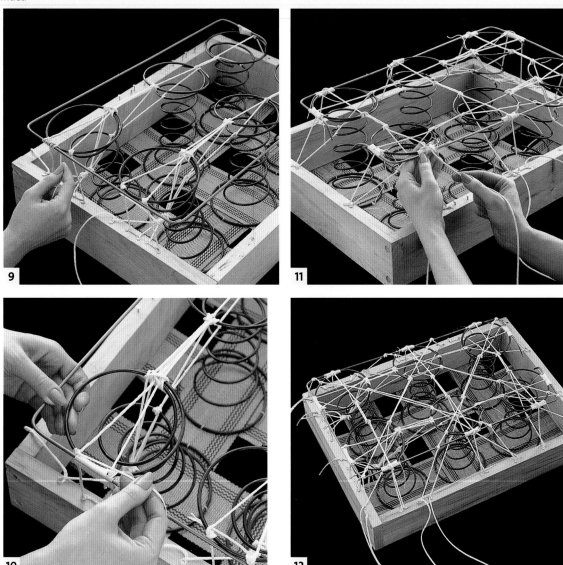

9. ALIGN edge wire to the outer edges of the top coils. Wrap doubled button twine repeatedly around the coil and edge wire, wrapping once outside the knot, then crossing over the knot and filling the space between knots, and then crossing the second knot and wrapping twice. Pack twines closely together in a singe layer.

10. WRAP twines between the spring and edge wire over previous wraps, pulling tight. Separate twines, and wrap them twice in opposite directions around the spring and edge wire, forming figure eights; tie the ends together, using two overhand knots.

11. REPEAT steps 8 to 10 at each spring. Set in nails for front side-to-side row, aligning nails to the center of the top coils. Tie side-to-side rows, following diagram (f) for the first twine and diagram (g) for the second twine; use clove hitch knots or overhand knots at each location for both twines, keeping all springs but the front row perpendicular to the webbing. Tie knots over any existing knots or loops.

12. MARK rails and prepare twines for diagonal rows as on page 37, step 8. Tie diagonal rows as in step 11, above, tying outer knots to the edge wire. Cut twine tails to about 3" (7.6 cm).

HOW TO COVER SPRINGS WITH BURLAP

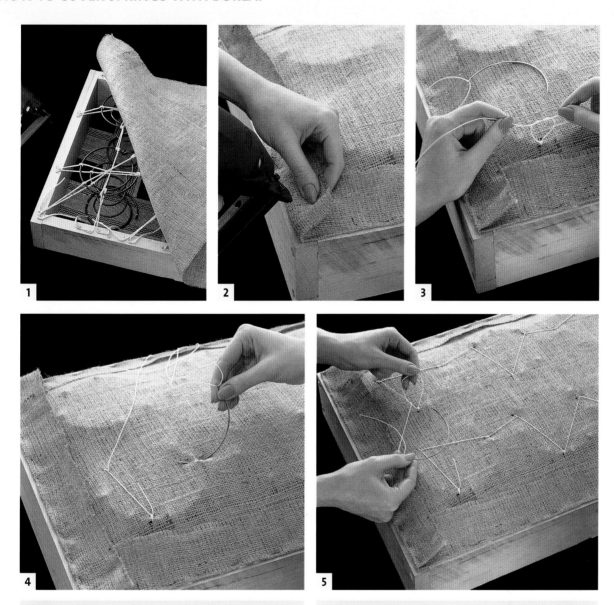

1. CUT burlap 3" (7.6 cm) larger than measurements from the outer edges of the rails, over the springs. Center burlap over the spring system. Staple burlap to the rails at the center front and center back, using 3/8" (1 cm) staples and pulling snug without compressing the springs. Repeat at the center sides.

2. FINISH stapling burlap on all sides, working from centers toward the corners. Fold out excess burlap at the corner; staple. Fold the raw edge of burlap back; staple again.

3. THREAD a 6" (15.2 cm) curved needle with nylon button twine. Beginning with a corner spring, insert the needle through the burlap, hooking the top coil. Take one short stitch, coming back through the burlap, leaving a tail for knotting. Secure the stitch with a slipknot. Tie an overhand knot over the slipknot.

4. STITCH burlap to the spring with two more evenly spaced stitches, arranging stitches so that the last stitch is located near the next spring. Secure each stitch with an overhand knot.

5. SECURE burlap to each spring with three stitches, working one entire row; proceed to the next row. Plan the stitch placement so that the last stitch on each spring is near the first stitch on the next spring. Lock all stitches between the first and last stitch with overhand knots; lock the last stitch with a slipknot, followed by two overhand knots.

DIAGRAMS FOR SPRING TYING

Follow these diagrams for tying springs so that, when completed, the springs in the system will work together as one unit. For a domed surface spring system, the top coils of the springs around the outer edges should angle toward the front, back, and side rails. For an edge wire spring system, the top coils should all form a flat surface even with the edge wire. If open-ended coil springs are used, the second knot on the back springs in diagram (c) should also secure the open end to the coil beneath it.

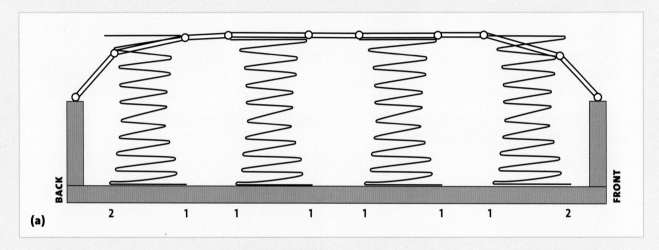

(a)

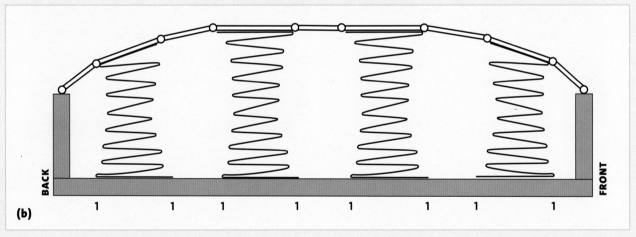

(b)

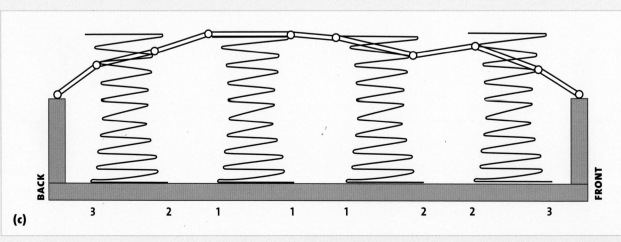

(c)

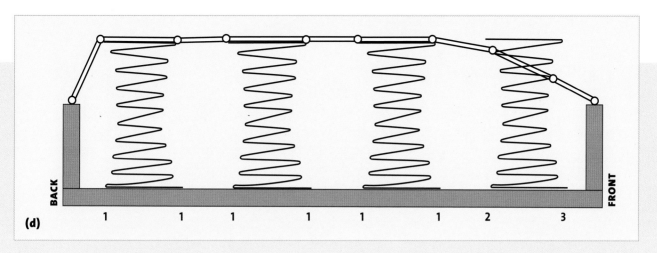

(d)

BACK 1 1 1 1 1 1 2 3 FRONT

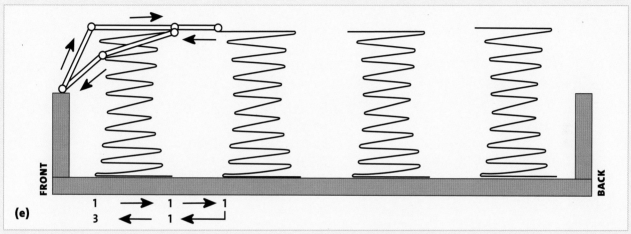

(e)

FRONT 1 1 1 | 3 1

BACK

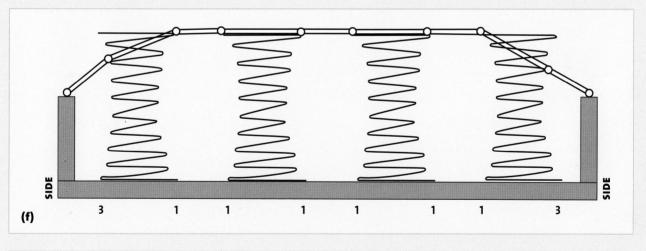

(f)

SIDE 3 1 1 1 1 1 3 SIDE

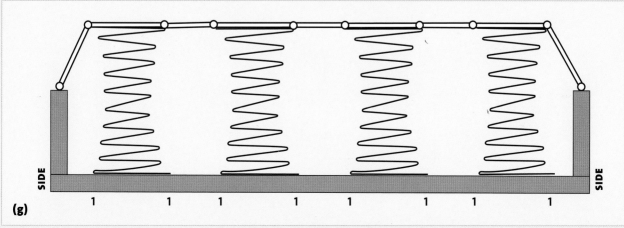

(g)

SIDE 1 1 1 1 1 1 1 SIDE

Welting

Fabric-covered cording, called *welting,* is both a decorative accent and a structural aspect of many upholstered pieces. Welting is attached along the lower edge of a chair to accent the edge and give it a clean finish. It is often sewn into the seam between two adjoining pieces or stapled to the chair frame between two adjoining pieces. While accenting the structural lines of the furniture piece, it also reduces wear and stress at these locations.

To conserve fabric, welting strips can be cut on the crosswise grain of the fabric. Since the resulting welting will be quite inflexible, use straight-grain welting only in places where it is applied to the furniture piece in a straight line. For welting applied in a curve, cut the strips on the bias, allowing the welting to bend without puckering. It is possible to use a combination of straight-grain and bias-grain welting in the same furniture piece, if the difference in grain cannot be detected.

Whenever possible, place welt seams and joints in inconspicuous places, such as the side of a cushion near a corner. Avoid placing them at the center of a section or on the front of the furniture.

Double welting is used as a decorative trim, often covering a raw fabric edge and staples or tacks. It is used in place of purchased trim, such as gimp.

TYPES OF WELTING

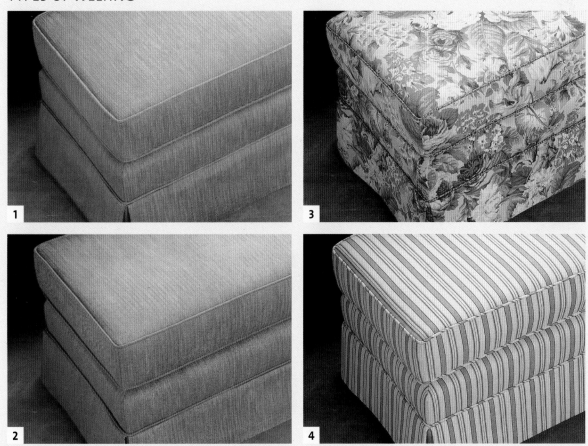

WELTING can be made from matching or contrasting fabric, depending on the look desired. Matching welting (1) gives the piece an overall uniform appearance. Contrasting welting (2) visually divides the piece into smaller sections and emphasized its design lines. Coordinating prints (3) or bias-cut stripes can be used to add creative interest to welted upholstery. If upholstering with a stripe or plaid, keep in mind that it will not always be possible to match the welting to the fabric. It is better to cut self-welting on the bias (4) or to use a solid color for the welting.

HOW TO MAKE WELTING FOR ATTACHING TO THE FRAME

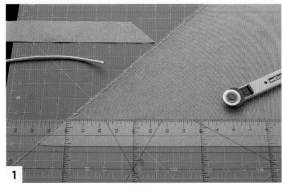

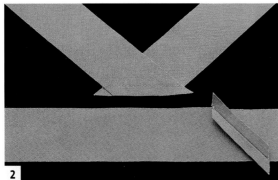

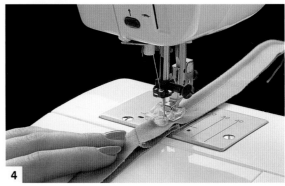

1. **Cut** fabric strips from the bias grain or crosswise grain, with the width equal to the circumference of the cording plus 1" (2.5 cm). Cut the short ends of strips at 45 degree angles for seaming.

2. **Stitch** the strips together as necessary for the desired length; press the seams open.

3. **Center** cording on the wrong side of the fabric strip; fold the strip around the cording, wrong sides together, matching raw edges and encasing the cord.

4. **Machine-baste** close to the cording, using a welting foot or zipper foot, to create welting.

HOW TO SEW WELTING INTO A SEAM

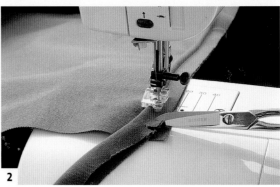

Continuous circle

1. **Follow** steps 1 to 3, above; align the cut edges of the welting strip to the cut edge of the fabric, beginning 3" (7.6 cm) from the end of the welting. Stitch close to the cording, using a welting foot or zipper foot.

2. **Stop** stitching 1¹/₂" (3.8 cm) from the corner. Clip welting seam allowances at the corner and again ¹/₂" (1.3 cm) behind the corner.

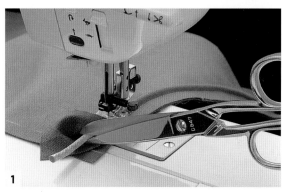

3

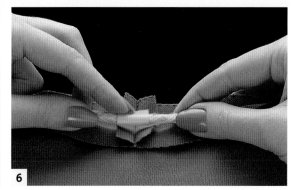

6

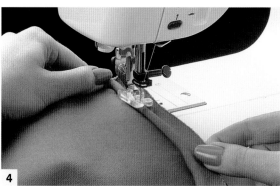

4

1

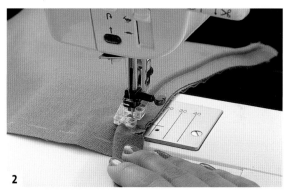

5

2

3. STITCH to the corner. Leave the needle down; raise the presser foot, and pivot. Pull the welting completely back against itself. Then realign the welting to the next edge. This will ensure that the welting doesn't pull in at the corner.

4. CONTINUE stitching 2" (5.1 cm) beyond the corner. Leave the needle down; raise the presser foot. Hold welting seam allowances taut; push your thumb into the welting corner, drawing more cording back to fill out the corner.

5. STOP stitching 3" (7.6 cm) from the point where the ends of the welting will meet. Overlap welting strip ends; mark with chalk across both welt strips. Cut off welting strip ends ½" (1.3 cm) beyond the marks.

6. STITCH the welt strip ends together at the marked lines; finger-press the seam open. Cut the cording so the ends butt. Wrap the cording joint with tape; tuck the cording back inside the welting. Finish sewing the welting to the fabric.

For welting that is crossed by a seam

1. STITCH welting to the edge of the fabric, stopping 1" (2.5 cm) behind the seam intersection. Cut off cording just behind the seam intersection. Slip the cording back into the welting strip.

2. NOTCH the welting seam allowance, starting ½" (1.3 cm) behind the seam intersection. Bend the welting down into the seam allowance, aligning the upper edge of the welting to the seam intersection point. Finish stitching the welting to the fabric, stitching across the empty welting.

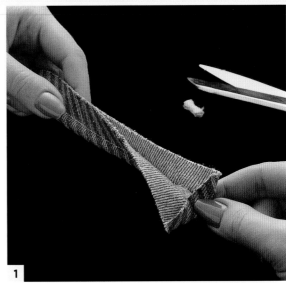

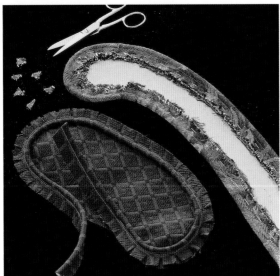

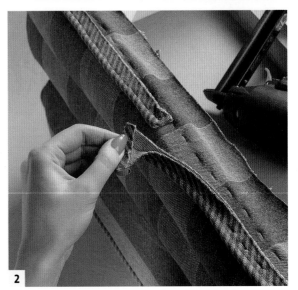

(top)

STRETCH welting slightly while stapling; slackness will cause rippling.

(bottom)

CLIP welting seam allowances when they lie outside curves, allowing welting to lie flat. Notch seam allowances when they lie inside curves and corners, reducing bulk.

Butt joint

1. REMOVE stitches 1" (2.5 cm) from the end of the welting. Open the casing; cut off the cording 1/2" (1.3 cm) from the end. Turn back fabric over the cording; refold, encasing the cording. Staple the welting in place.

2. STOP stapling 4" to 5" (10.2 to 12.7 cm) from the joint. Cut off welting 1/2" (1.3 cm) beyond the joint; remove stitches 1" (2.5 cm) from the end of the welting. Open the casing; cut off the cording 1/2" (1.3 cm) from the end. Turn back fabric over the cording; refold, encasing the cording. Staple the welting in place, butting the ends tightly together.

HOW TO MAKE DOUBLE WELTING

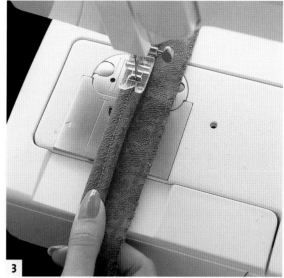

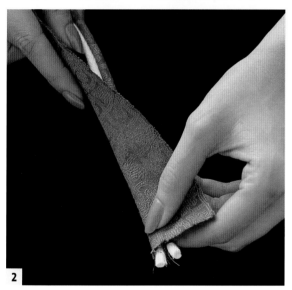

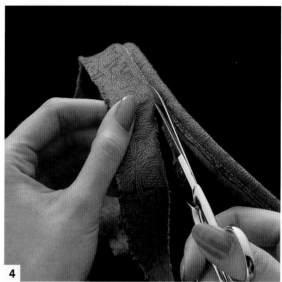

1. Place ⁵/₃₂" (3.8 mm) cording on the wrong side of a 3" (7.6 cm) fabric strip. Fold fabric over the cording, with a ¹/₂" (1.3 cm) seam allowance extending. Stitch next to the cording, using a welting foot or zipper foot.

2. Place the second cording next to the first welt. Wrap fabric around the second cording.

3. Stitch between the two cords on the previous stitching line. Use a general-purpose foot, riding on top of the welting.

4. Trim off excess fabric next to the stitching; the raw edge is on the back of the finished double welting.

Cushions found on chairs, sofas, and ottomans vary in construction method and design.

Three basic styles of cushions are boxed (1), waterfall (2), and knife-edge (3). Any of these may be fitted flush to the front of the chair or T-shaped, wrapping around the front of the chair arms. Boxed cushions can be sewn with or without welting at the top and bottom seams. Knife-edge cushions usually have a welted seam around the center on sides where the cushion is exposed. Hidden sides are often constructed with a boxing strip. Waterfall cushions, common in contemporary furniture, are sewn with one continuous piece of fabric wrapping over the front, from top to bottom. This style has a boxing strip around the sides and back and is usually constructed without welting.

As a general rule, the finished width of the boxing strip is 3/4" (1.9 cm) narrower than the height of the foam. Many waterfall cushions, however, are made with narrower boxing strips. The fabric wraps over the sides from the top and bottom and forms small pleats around the curved front of the boxing strip. To copy this type of cushion cover, it is best to make a pattern off the original cushion.

Chair and sofa cushions are generally constructed with a zipper closure centered in the boxing strip that wraps around the back corners of the cushion. This allows for easier insertion of the cushion into its cover. Because the cushions must be shaped to conform to the back and sides of the chair or sofa, it is necessary to tailor a pattern before cutting the fabric. The pattern-tailoring instructions given are for single chair cushions. However, patterns for multiple sofa cushions are tailored in the same manner, marking the dividing line between cushions on the sofa deck and then making a separate pattern for each cushion.

Cushions that are exposed on all sides, such as ottoman cushions, are hand-sewn closed. These rectangular cushions, generally boxed or knife-edge, do not need a tailored pattern.

BOXED CUSHIONS

CUTTING DIRECTIONS

Cut a cushion top and a cushion bottom, using the pattern tailored on page 52, steps 1 to 4. If making a rectangular cushion, exposed on all sides, cut a cushion top and a cushion bottom, with the length and width equal to the desired finished length and width plus 1" (2.5 cm). If the cushion will be welted, cut fabric strips for the welting (page 45), with the length equal to twice the circumference of the cushion plus additional length for seaming strips, joining ends, and inconspicuously positioning seams.

Cut the boxing strip. If the original cushion insert will be used, measure the width of the original boxing strip between the seams and add 1" (2.5 cm) for seam allowances. If a new cushion insert will be prepared, cut the boxing strip 1/4" (6 mm) wider than the foam thickness. For a cushion that will be sewn closed, the cut length of the boxing strip is equal to the finished circumference of the cushion plus 1" (2.5 cm) for seam allowances. If seaming will be necessary, allow 1" (2.5 cm) for each seam, planning for inconspicuous placement.

For a cushion with a zipper closure, cut the boxing strip with the length equal to the measurement of the front and sides of the cushion. Excess length will be cut off during construction. If seaming will be necessary, allow 1" (2.5 cm) for each seam, planning the placement of the seams out of view along the sides of the cushion. If continuous zipper tape is used, cut the zipper tape with the length equal to the back cushion measurement plus 8" (20.3 cm), or purchase an upholstery zipper with this approximate length. Cut two fabric strips for the zipper closure, with the length of the strips equal to the length of the zipper tape and the width of the strips equal to half the cut width of the boxing strip plus 3/4" (1.9 cm).

YOU WILL NEED

- Muslin
- Upholstery fabric
- Welt cording and fabric
- Upholstery zipper or continuous zipper tape and zipper pull
- Foam
- Polyester batting and spray foam adhesive, or button needle and heavy thread

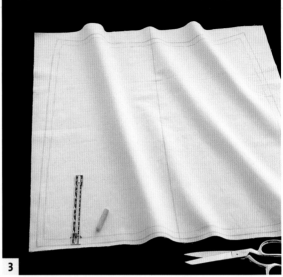

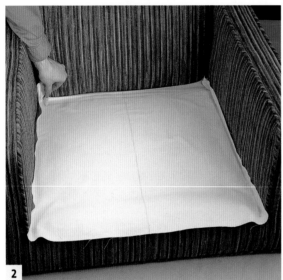

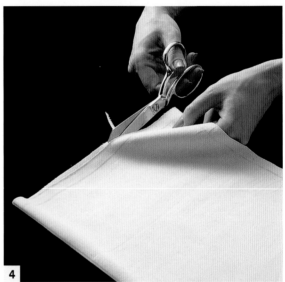

1. **MEASURE** the seat opening in both directions at the widest point; add 2" (5.1 cm) to each measurement. Cut muslin to this size; mark a centerline from the front to back. Center muslin over the chair deck, turning excess muslin up along the arms and back. For a T-cushion, clip muslin around the curves, allowing it to lie flat.

2. **MARK** an outline of the cushion, holding a sharpened stick of chalk perpendicular to the deck and following the shape of the inside arms and back of the chair; the chalk should brush against but not push into the chair padding. Mark the cushion front along the crown of the nosing.

3. **REMOVE** the muslin. Draw a ¹/₂" (1.3 cm) seam allowance outside the marked line; cut out the pattern.

4. **FOLD** the pattern in half on the centerline, checking to see that the pattern is symmetrical. Trim edges even if they are off by less than 1" (2.5 cm); unfold the pattern. If the edges are off by more than 1" (2.5 cm), adjust the chair padding and draw the new pattern.

HOW TO SEW A BOXED CUSHION COVER WITH A ZIPPER

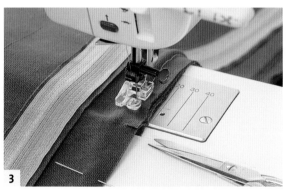

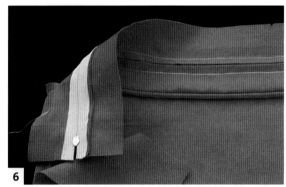

1. SEW welting around the outer edges of the cushion top and cushion bottom, following the continuous circle method on pages 46 and 47, steps 1 to 6.

2. PRESS under a 3/4" (1.9 cm) seam allowance on one long edge of the zipper strip. Position the folded edge of the strip along the center of the zipper teeth, right sides up. Using a zipper foot, topstitch 3/4" (1.9 cm) from the fold. Repeat for the opposite side, making sure folds meet at the center of the zipper. If using continuous zipper tape, attach a zipper pull to the tape.

3. CENTER the zipper strip over the back of the cushion top. Stitch the zipper strip to the cushion top, beginning and ending on sides about 1 1/2" (3.8 cm) beyond the corners; clip once into the zipper strip seam allowance at each corner, and pivot.

4. ALIGN the center of the boxing strip to the front center of the cushion top, matching print, if necessary; pin-mark the pieces separately. Smooth the boxing strip to the right front corner; mark with a 3/8" (1 cm) clip into the seam allowance. Smooth the boxing strip along the right side of the cushion top; pin the boxing strip to the cushion top about 6" (15.2 cm) from the back corner.

5. STITCH the boxing strip to the cushion top, beginning at the side pin and sewing a 1/2" (1.3 cm) seam. For a welted cushion, use a welting foot or zipper foot. Match the clip mark to the front corner; pivot stitching at the corner.

6. CONTINUE stitching the boxing strip to the cushion top, matching the center marks. Clip once into the boxing strip seam allowance at the left front corner; pivot. Stop stitching about 6" (15.2 cm) from the back left corner.

continued on next page

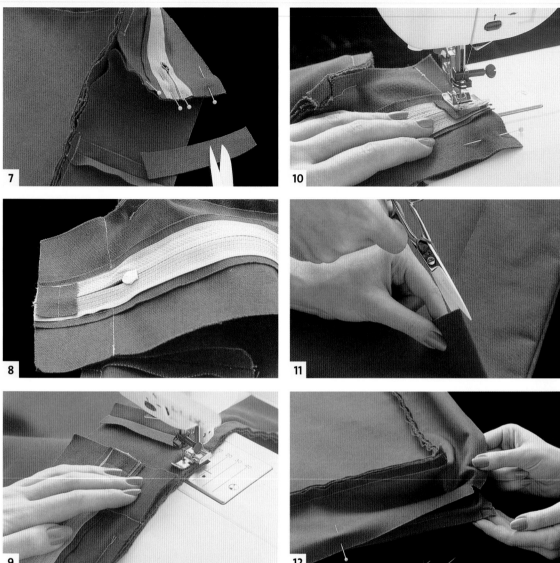

7. CUT the boxing strip 4" (10.2 cm) beyond the point where it overlaps the zipper pull end of the zipper strip. Pin the end of the boxing strip to the end of the zipper strip, right sides together, matching all cut edges.

8. STITCH together 2" (5.1 cm) from the end; pivot at the zipper tape. Stitch along the outer edge of the zipper tape to within ½" (1.3 cm) of the end; pivot. Place a small scrap of fabric over the zipper teeth. Stitch slowly across the teeth to the opposite side of the zipper tape, taking care not to break the needle; pivot. Stitch along the opposite side of the zipper tape until 2" (5.1 cm) from the end; pivot, and stitch to the edge.

9. FINGER-PRESS the seam allowance toward the boxing strip; finish sewing the zipper strip and boxing strip to the cushion top. A small pocket forms to hide the zipper pull when closed.

10. CUT the opposite end of the boxing strip 1" (2.5 cm) beyond the point where it overlaps the end of the zipper strip. Pin the ends together. Stitch ½" (1.3 cm) from the ends, placing a scrap of fabric over the zipper teeth and stitching slowly. Turn the seam allowance toward the boxing strip; finish sewing the zipper strip and boxing strip to the cushion top.

11. FOLD the boxing strip straight across at the corner; mark the opposite side of the boxing strip with a ³/₈" (1 cm) clip into the seam allowance. Repeat for all of the corners.

12. OPEN the zipper partially. Pin the boxing strip to the cushion bottom, matching clip marks to the corners. Stitch. Turn right side out through the zipper opening.

HOW TO SEW A BOXED CUSHION COVER WITHOUT A ZIPPER

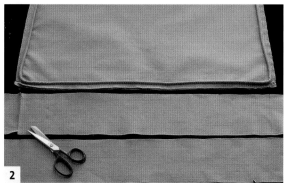

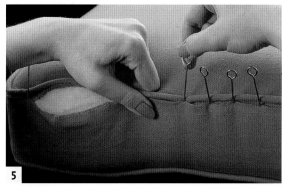

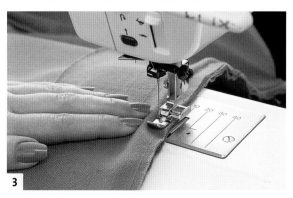

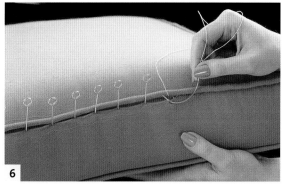

1. FOLLOW step 1 on page 53. Sew the boxing strip sections together as necessary.

2. CHECK to see that the boxing strip fits the cushion top. Mark the boxing strip at the corners with 3/8" (1 cm) clips into the seam allowance. Fold the boxing strip straight across at the marks; clip-mark the opposite side of the boxing strip.

3. PIN the boxing strip to the cushion top, matching clip marks to the corners; stitch a 1/2" (1.3 cm) seam. Use a welting foot or zipper foot if the cushion is welted.

4. PIN the boxing strip to the cushion bottom, matching clip marks to the corners; stitch a 1/2" (1.3 cm) seam, leaving the back side open for inserting the cushion. Backstitch at the beginning and end of the seam.

5. PREPARE and insert the cushion (pages 59 to 61). Fold back the boxing strip seam allowance along the opening, overlapping the cushion bottom seam allowance 1/2" (1.3 cm); pin. Compress the cushion along the open side for easier pinning.

6. BLINDSTITCH (page 69) the opening closed, using the 3" (7.6 cm) curved needle and heavy thread. Begin and end the stitching 1" (2.5 cm) beyond the opening; knot securely.

WATERFALL CUSHIONS

CUTTING DIRECTIONS

Cut a cushion top and bottom piece, using the pattern tailored in steps 1 to 3, right and below. Mark the end of the piece that will become the cushion top; with a directional print or napped fabric, the fabric will run in the correct direction only on the top.

Cut the side boxing strips. If the original cushion insert will be used, measure the width of the original boxing strip between the seams and add 1" (2.5 cm) for seam allowances. If a new cushion insert will be prepared, cut the boxing strips 1/4" (6 mm) wider than the foam thickness. Cut each boxing strip with the length equal to the side measurement of the cushion plus 1" (2.5 cm). Excess length will be cut off during construction. If continuous zipper tape is used, cut the zipper tape with the length equal to the back cushion measurement plus 8" (20.3 cm), or purchase an upholstery zipper with this approximate length. Cut two fabric strips for the zipper closure, with the length of the strips equal to the length of the zipper tape and the width of the strips equal to half the cut width of the boxing strip plus 3/4" (1.9 cm).

HOW TO TAILOR A PATTERN FOR A WATERFALL CUSHION

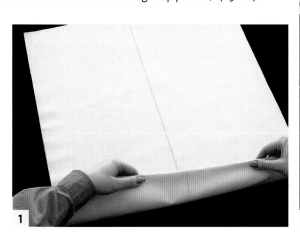

1. MEASURE the seat opening in both directions at the widest points. Multiply the depth by two and add the cushion height. Add 4" (10.2 cm) to the depth and 2" (5.1 cm) to the width measurements; cut muslin to this size. Mark a centerline through the entire length. Fold the fabric in half, perpendicular to the centerline; crease.

2. DRAW a line across the width of muslin a distance above the fold equal to half the cushion height. Unfold the muslin. Center one end of the muslin over the chair deck, aligning the marked line to the crown of the nosing and turning excess muslin up along the arms and back. For a T-cushion, clip muslin around the curves, allowing it to lie flat.

3. FOLLOW steps 2 to 4 on page 52. Fold under the uncut end of the pattern along the crosswise crease; cut the lower layer to match the cutting line of the upper layer. Mark the lower layer even with the nosing line; unfold the pattern.

HOW TO SEW A WATERFALL CUSHION COVER

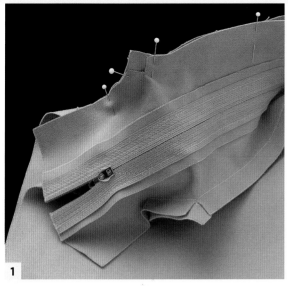

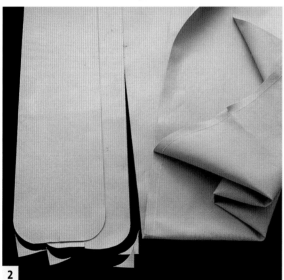

1. Follow steps 2 and 3 on page 53. Fold the zipper strip straight across at the corner; mark the opposite edge with a 3/8" (1 cm) clip into the seam allowance. Repeat at the other corner. Pin the zipper strip to the cushion bottom, matching clip marks to the corners. Stitch, beginning and ending about 1 1/2" (3.8 cm) beyond the corners.

2. Mark the center of the front short end of each side of the boxing strip; round the front corners of the side boxing strips slightly. Mark the outer edges of the top and bottom cushion piece even with the crosswise crease of the pattern. Staystitch a scant 1/2" (1.3 cm) from the outer edges of the piece a distance on either side of the marks equal to the cushion height.

3. Clip the seam allowances to staystitching every 1/2" (1.3 cm). Pin the side boxing strip to the cushion piece, right sides together, aligning the center marks. Check to see that the corresponding points on the top and bottom match up directly across from each other on the boxing strip. Sew a 1/2" (1.3 cm) seam, beginning and ending 6" (15.2 cm) from the back corners. Repeat for the opposite side.

4. Follow steps 7 to 10 on page 54. Open the zipper partially. Finish sewing the boxing strip to the cushion bottom on both sides. Turn the cushion cover right side out through the zipper opening.

KNIFE-EDGE CUSHIONS

CUTTING DIRECTIONS

Cut a cushion top and a cushion bottom, using the pattern tailored below for a fitted chair or sofa cushion. If the cushion is exposed on all four sides, cut two rectangles of fabric, with the width and length equal to the finished width and length of the cushion plus the foam height plus 1/4" (6 mm). Cut fabric strips for the welting (page 45), with the length equal to the length of the knife-edge section of the cushion cover.

Cut the side boxing strips. If the original cushion insert will be used, measure the width of the original boxing strip between the seams and add 1" (2.5 cm) for seam allowances. If a new cushion insert will be prepared, cut the boxing strips

1/4" (6 mm) wider than the foam thickness. Cut the boxing strips with the length equal to the measurement of the side of the cushion. Excess length will be cut off during construction. If continuous zipper tape is used, cut the zipper tape with the length equal to the back cushion measurement plus 8" (20.3 cm), or purchase an upholstery zipper with this approximate length. Cut two fabric strips for the zipper closure, with the length of the strips equal to the length of the zipper tape and the width of the strips equal to half the cut width of the boxing strip plus 3/4" (1.9 cm).

HOW TO TAILOR A PATTERN FOR A KNIFE-EDGE CUSHION

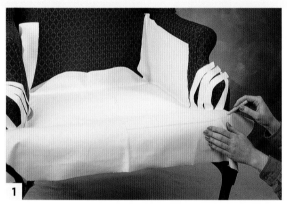

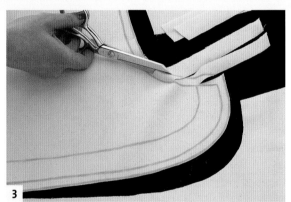

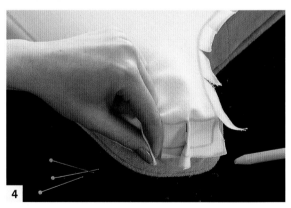

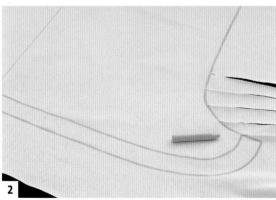

1. FOLLOW steps 1 and 2 on page 52, adding the cushion height plus 2" (5.1 cm) to the seat measurements before cutting the muslin. Remove the muslin.

2. DRAW a line along the front of the cushion pattern a distance from the marked line equal to half the finished boxing height. For a T-cushion, extend the line around the front corners to a point even with the line at the back of the T; connect the ends of the lines.

3. DRAW a 1/2" (1.3 cm) seam allowance outside the entire pattern; cut out the pattern. Follow step 4 on page 52.

4. LAY the pattern over the original cushion, aligning the pattern seam line to the midpoint of the cushion height; pin out corner tucks. Mark tucks; unfold the pattern. Transfer marks to the opposite corner.

HOW TO SEW A KNIFE-EDGE CUSHION COVER

1

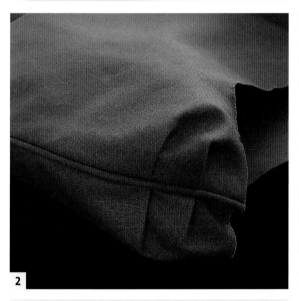

2

1. Fold out the corner tucks on the cushion top and bottom; baste. Sew the welting to the desired edges of the cushion top, following the method for welting that is crossed by a seam on page 47, for a tailored cushion, or the continuous circle method on pages 46 and 47, for totally knife-edged cushion.

2. Pin the cushion bottom to the cushion top along the welted edge, matching the corner tucks. Stitch the seam, crowding the cording. For totally knife-edged cushion, leave one side open for inserting the cushion; hand-stitch closed. For a tailored cushion, complete the cushion cover as for the waterfall cushion on page 57, steps 1 to 4.

HOW TO PREPARE AND INSERT THE CUSHION

1

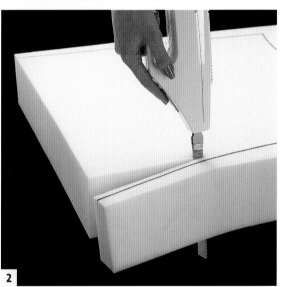

2

1. Trace the cutting line of the cushion cover onto the foam, using a marker.

2. Cut the foam, using an electric knife. Follow the seam line of the pattern for high-resiliency foam; follow the cutting line for softer foam. Hold the knife blade perpendicular to the foam at all times.

continued on next page

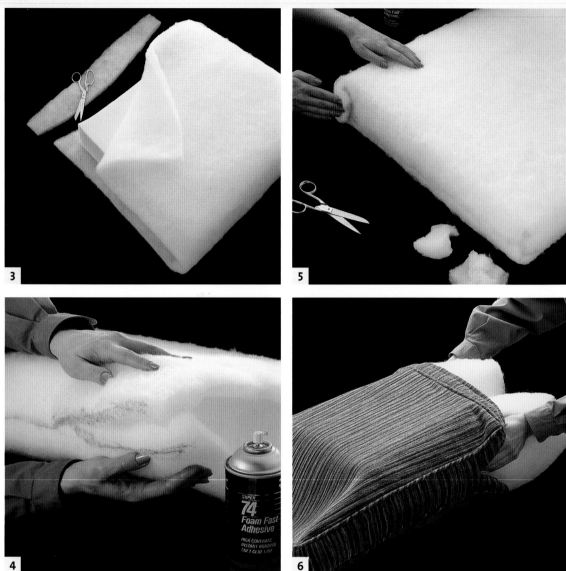

3. WRAP polyester batting over the foam from front to back. Trim the sides and back so that the cut edges overlap about 1" (2.5 cm) at the center of the cushion.

4. APPLY spray foam adhesive to the cut edges of the batting at the back of the cushion; overlap the edges, and press firmly to seal, forming a smooth seam. Or whipstitch the edges together, using a button needle and heavy thread. Repeat for the sides.

5. TRIM excess batting vertically at the back corners, for a fitted cushion. Fold back excess batting over the side seams at the front corners of a fitted cushion or all corners of a rectangular cushion. Apply adhesive; press together firmly to seal. Or whipstitch the corners in place.

6. FOLD the cushion in half from the front to back. Insert the cushion into the opening, gradually working the cushion toward the front of the cover. Stretch the cover to fit the cushion.

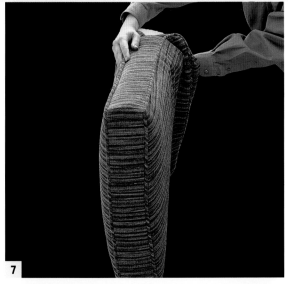

7

1

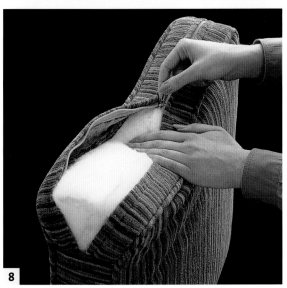

8

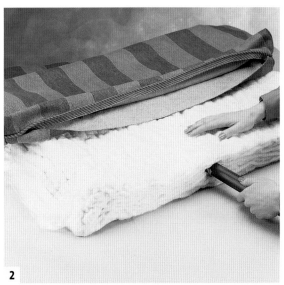

2

7. STAND the cushion on one side. Check to see that the cushion is inserted symmetrically, with equal fullness on both sides; adjust, if necessary.

8. TURN the seam allowances toward the boxing strip all around the cushion. Zip closed, hiding the zipper pull in the pocket. Or hand-stitch closed (page 55).

1. INSERT the prepared cushion into a lightweight trash bag, or wrap with lightweight plastic. Overlap the open edges of plastic at one end. Insert a vacuum hose into a small hole cut in the plastic bag, or wrap plastic around the hose; hold tightly.

2. PLACE the end of the hose against the cushion. Turn on the vacuum. Suck air from the cushion until it slips easily into the cover. Turn off the vacuum; remove the plastic, allowing air to reenter the cushion.

Skirts

The final upholstery step for many furniture pieces is attaching a skirt around the bottom. Skirts add a decorative touch while also hiding plain legs and visually anchoring the furniture.

Skirt styles vary, depending on the design of the furniture and the look desired. The most common skirt style is a tailored, flat panel with kick pleats at the corners (1). With this skirt style, the fabric pattern can be matched in a continuous flow to the floor. On larger pieces, such as a sofa, the tailored skirt may have one or two kick pleats along the front panel, aligned to the cushion breaks. Other skirt styles feature open box pleats (2) or closed box pleats (3) spaced evenly and continuously around the bottom. For a country or feminine look, the skirt can be gathered (4). This style requires lightweight upholstery fabric.

The skirt is sewn to welting that fits tightly around the furniture. The entire skirt is then either hand-sewn or stapled in place. Though hand sewing seems more difficult and time-consuming, it results in a very attractive, secure finish. Stapling is only possible if the welt rests over unpadded or lightly padded wood.

Skirt length is very critical. Measure for the length with the furniture standing on a hard surface. The skirt hem should be $1/2$" to 1" (1.3 to 2.5 cm) above the surface, if the furniture will be placed on a hard floor. If the furniture will be placed on a carpeted floor, depending on the depth of the pile, the skirt hem should be 1" to $1^1/2$" (2.5 to 3.8 cm) above the surface.

The placement for the upper welted edge of the skirt is usually determined by the original skirt placement. However, this can often be altered if a different look is desired. In general, the skirt should be at least 6" (15.2 cm) long. It may be helpful to pin a mock skirt at different heights to decide on the most appealing placement. Matching furniture pieces, such as a chair and ottoman, should always have matching skirts.

Cutting Directions

For all skirt styles, cut fabric strips for the welting (page 45), with the length equal to the circumference of the furniture piece at the placement line for the upper edge of the skirt plus additional length for seaming strips, joining ends, and inconspicuously positioning seams.

For a flat-panel skirt, measure and record the widths of the front, back, and sides of the furniture piece, measuring along the skirt placement line as drawn on page 64, step 5. For a

sofa, measure and record the distances from the corners to the first cushion breaks and the distance between any additional cushion breaks. Cut a separate piece of fabric for each section of the skirt, with the width equal to the measured width of the section plus 8" (20.3 cm). The cut length of each section is equal to the desired finished length of the skirt from the welt seam to the hem plus $1^1/2$" (3.8 cm). Follow the pattern-matching guidelines on page 22 for cutting patterned fabric.

Cut a piece of fabric, 8" (20.3 cm) wide, for the underpanel of each kick pleat, with the length of each piece equal to the cut length of the skirt sections.

Cut lining pieces equal in width to each skirt section and underpanel; the cut length of the lining pieces is 1" (2.5 cm) shorter than the cut length of the skirt.

Cut buckram pieces for each skirt section and underpanel, with the cut width equal to the finished width of the section minus $1/2$" (1.3 cm) and the cut length equal to the finished length of the skirt minus $3/4$" (1.9 cm).

For a box-pleated or gathered skirt, measure the circumference of the furniture piece, measuring along the skirt placement line as drawn on page 64, step 5. Cut fabric pieces with the total cut width, after seaming, of two-and-one-half times this measurement for open box pleats or gathers or three times this measurement for closed box pleats. The cut length of the pieces is equal to the desired finished length of the skirt from the welting seam to the hem plus $1^1/2$" (3.8 cm).

Cut lining equal in width, after seaming, to the cut width of the skirt, railroading (page 17) the lining to eliminate some seams, if possible. The cut length of the lining is 1" (2.5 cm) shorter than the cut length of the skirt.

You Will Need

- Upholstery fabric

- Lining fabric, such as lightweight denim

- Buckram

- Welt cording

- Chalk

- #3 curved needle and heavy thread, or staple gun and $3/8$" (1 cm) staples

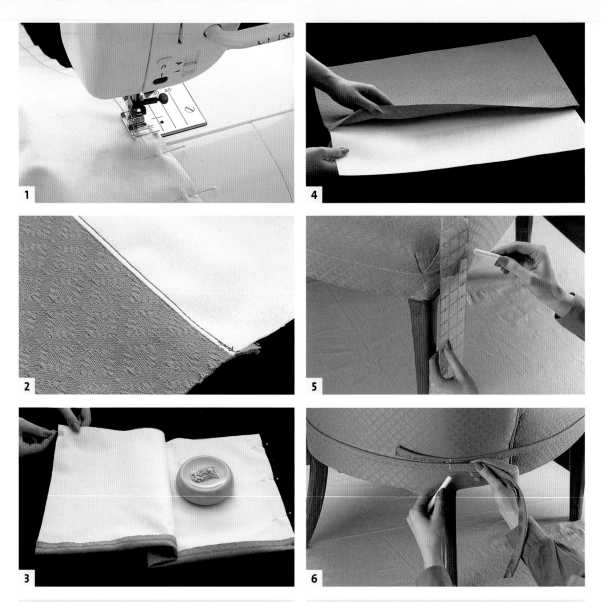

1. PIN lining to the lower edge of one skirt section, matching cut edges; stitch a $1/2$" (1.3 cm) seam.

2. PRESS the seam allowances toward the lining. Understitch on the right side of the lining, close to the seam line, stitching through the lining and both seam allowances.

3. PIN the lining and fabric, right sides together, at the ends; align the upper and side edges. Skirt fabric will roll $1/2$" (1.3 cm) toward the lining side. Stitch a $1/2$" (1.3 cm) seam. Repeat for the opposite end.

4. TURN the skirt section right side out, aligning the upper edges; press. Insert buckram between the skirt and the lining, aligning the lower edge of the buckram to the bottom of the skirt. Baste the upper edges of the skirt and lining together within the $1/2$" (1.3 cm) seam allowance.

5. REPEAT steps 1 to 4 for all skirt sections and pleat underpanels. Determine the placement for the top of the skirt; mark with chalk at the height of the welting seam, measuring up from the floor. Make welting as on page 46, steps 1 to 4.

6. WRAP the welting tightly around the furniture at the marked line, lapping ends at the back; pin. Check to see that the welting seams are placed inconspicuously. Pin-mark welting at the corners and at the cushion breaks, if any. Mark the ends at the overlap.

7

9

8

10

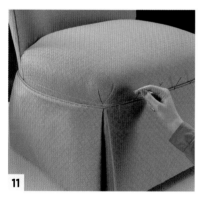

11

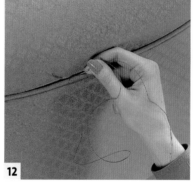

12

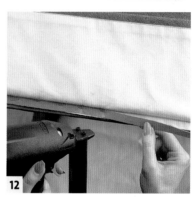

12

7. REMOVE the welting. Cut off the welting strip ends $^1/_2$" (1.3 cm) beyond the marks. Join ends as on page 47, step 6; sew the welting closed, forming a circle.

8. FOLD under $3^1/_2$" (8.9 cm) at the ends of the front skirt panel. Pin welting to the panel, aligning the seam allowances and matching the front pin marks to the folds. Adjust the depth of the folds, if necessary. Stitch, welting side up, using a welting foot or zipper foot and crowding the cording. Repeat for each skirt section.

9. PRESS the folds. Center the pleat underpanel over the folds at one corner, right sides down. Shift the underpanel upward, $^1/_4$" to $^3/_8$" (6 mm to 1 cm) beyond the upper edges of the skirt and the welting seam allowance; stitch.

10. TURN the welting seam allowance toward the kick pleat; check to see that the lower edge of the underpanel is even with or slightly shorter than the lower edges of the corner folds. Adjust, if necessary. Repeat step 9 for the remaining kick pleats, shifting the underpanel the same distance as for the first corner.

11. SLIP the skirt onto the furniture from the bottom, first over the back legs and then over the front. Turn down the upper seam allowances; align the welting seam line to the marked line on the furniture; pin.

12. BLINDSTITCH (page 69) the skirt to the furniture, using a #3 curved needle and heavy thread, stitching into the welting seam.

Stapled method

12. TURN the skirt up. Place a tack strip over the seam allowances, aligning the upper edge of the tack strip to the seam line. Staple in place.

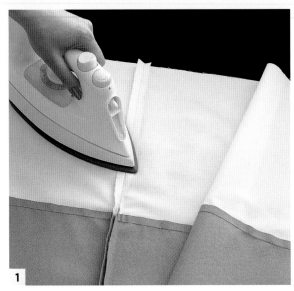

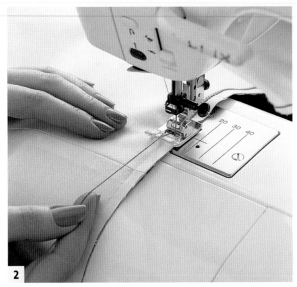

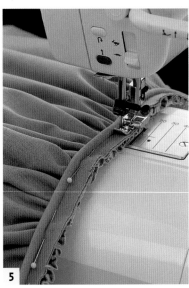

1. SEAM the skirt and lining as necessary to obtain the desired cut width; press the seam allowances open. Sew the lining to the skirt as on page 64, steps 1 and 2. Sew the ends, right sides together, making a continuous circle; press the seam allowances open.

2. FOLD the skirt, wrong sides together, aligning the upper cut edges; baste within the ¹/₂" (1.3 cm) seam allowance, taking care not to let the layers shift. Zigzag over a cord within the seam allowance on the back side of the skirt. Mark the furniture and prepare the welting as on pages 64 and 65, steps 5 to 7.

3. MEASURE the distance between the two welting pin marks, beginning at a back corner. Pin-mark the upper edge of the skirt, measuring two-and-one-half times this distance; place the first pin about 3" (7.6 cm) from the seam. Repeat for all pin-marked sections; the measurements on the skirt need not be exact.

4. PIN the welting to the right side of the skirt, matching pin marks. Pull on the gathering cord, and gather the skirt evenly to fit the welting.

5. SEW the welting to the skirt, using a welting foot or zipper foot. Attach the skirt to the furniture as on page 65, steps 11 and 12.

HOW TO SEW A PLEATED SKIRT

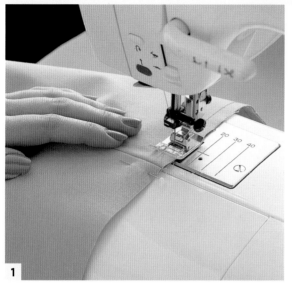

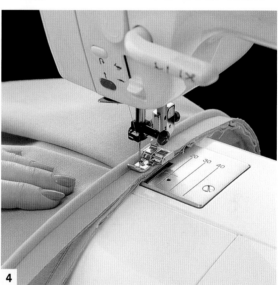

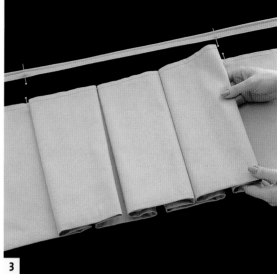

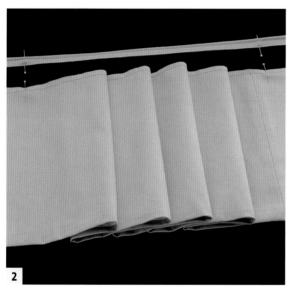

1. PREPARE the skirt as in step 1, opposite. Fold the skirt, wrong sides together, aligning the upper cut edges; baste within the 1/2" (1.3 cm) seam allowance, taking care not to let the layers shift.

2. MEASURE the distance between two welting pin marks, beginning at a back corner. Pin-mark the upper edge of the skirt, measuring two-and-one-half times this distance for open box pleats or three times this distance for closed box pleats; place the first pin about 2" (5.1 cm) from the seam. Repeat for all pin-marked sections; the measurements on the skirt need not be exact.

3. DETERMINE the desired size and spacing of pleats. Fold out the pleats, hiding any seams in the folds of the pleats. For open box pleats, the pleat sequence on the front and back begins and ends with a fold; the pleat sequence on sides begins and ends with a space. For closed box pleats, position the folds at all corners.

4. PIN the welting to the skirt, matching pin marks on the welting to the skirt corners; stitch, using a welting foot or zipper foot. Attach the skirt to the furniture as on page 65, steps 11 and 12.

Fitting & Finishing Techniques

Molding flat pieces of fabric over padded curves while circumventing numerous rails and posts is not a hit-or-miss procedure. Upholstery is actually a methodical craft, which, once understood, makes perfect sense. The secret to achieving professional results lies in the correct application of a few basic upholstery techniques.

STITCH *stretchers,* strips of strong, inexpensive fabric, to the edges of a cover section that will be hidden, conserving upholstery fabric. Turn seam allowances toward the stretcher; edgestitch. Attach the section to the furniture frame as usual, making necessary cuts and stapling through the stretchers.

STAPLE-BASTE the cover fabric to hold it in place temporarily, while working in another area. Hold the staple gun just above the surface; drive the staple partway into the frame, allowing it to be easily removed before final stapling.

STEAM the newly upholstered furniture, shrinking out any minute puckers and tightening the cover for a taut, firm appearance.

HAND-STITCH AROUND THE FRONT ARM BAND OF A ROLLED ARM, USING SMALL, EVENLY SPACED RUNNING STITCHES. PULL UP ON THREAD TO PLEAT OUT FABRIC EVENLY; STAPLE.

Pleat out excess fabric to make the cover fit smoothly around convex curves, such as the rounded back of an overstuffed chair. Use a regulator (page 10) to form sharp pleats.

Prevent pull marks by stapling just behind, rather than directly over, the spot being pulled. Stapling through padding also produces pull marks.

Relief-cut the edge of the cover fabric with a series of cuts, allowing it to mold smoothly around a concave curve, such as the inward arc of a wing. Make the cuts shallow enough so that they will be covered by an adjoining cover section, but deep enough to be effective. Depending on the location and shape of the curve, the relief cuts may consist of evenly spaced clips along the cut edge (1) or a series of clips that branch off from each other (2).

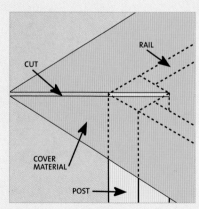

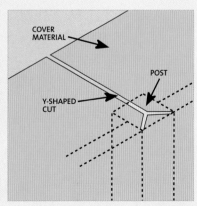

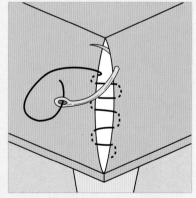

Diagonal-cut the cover fabric, allowing it to wrap around the opposite sides of a corner post. Measure before cutting to ensure that the cut will end at the inside corner of the post. Fold under cut edges even with the post sides; pull taut, and staple to rails.

Y-cut the cover fabric, allowing it to wrap around the opposite sides of a post or rail that is not at a corner. The width of the Y is equal to the width of the post or rail. Measure before cutting to ensure that the cut will end at the face of the post or rail.

Blindstitch adjoining sections together when other methods of attachment are not suitable. Use a curved needle to stitch in and out of the adjoining pieces, once they are pinned in place.

Upholstery
PROJECTS

SLIP SEATS

Upholstered seats on dining room or kitchen chairs are often referred to as slip seats. Because they are so easy to remove and reupholster, slip seats are a good choice for a beginning project. Whether the seat is worn or soiled, or if you simply want to change the fabric to coordinate with the room, a set of four chairs can easily be reupholstered in a day.

Most slip seats are made of a thin board, usually padded with foam and polyester batting. Another style of slip seat consists of an open wooden framework with a webbed top. The webbing is covered with burlap, and the seat may be padded with either horsehair and cotton batting or foam and polyester batting. If the padding is in good condition and the webbing is still taut, the chair seat can be reupholstered simply by removing the outer cover and attaching new fabric, as on page 74, steps 4 to 10. If the webbing is slack, the padding must be removed and the seat rewebbed (page 28). New foam and polyester batting can be attached, as on page 74, steps 2 and 3.

The slip seats of some chair styles drop into a recess in the chair seat. Other styles rest directly on the surface of the seat and may have welting attached around the lower edge. All styles are held in place by screws attached from the underside of the seat. Regardless of the style, if more than one chair in a set is being reupholstered, it is important to return seats to their original chairs, assuring proper fit and alignment of screw holes.

CUTTING DIRECTIONS

Cut the fabric 6" (15.2 cm) larger than the length and width of the chair seat. If new padding is needed, cut the foam 1" (2.5 cm) larger than the length and width of the chair seat. Cut the batting roughly 4" (10.2 cm) larger than the length and width of the chair seat. Cut the cambric 2" (5.1 cm) larger than the chair seat.

For the welting at the bottom of the chair seat, cut fabric strips 1½" (3.8 cm) wide on either the bias or crosswise grain; the combined length of the strips is equal to the distance around the chair seat plus extra for seam allowances and butt joint.

YOU WILL NEED

- Screwdriver and tack lifter or staple remover

- Foam, 1" (2.5 cm) thick

- Foam adhesive

- Polyester upholstery batting, 27" (68.6 cm) wide; 3 yd. (2.75 m) for four chair seats

- Upholstery fabric

- Staple gun and staples, ⅜" (1 cm)

- Welt cording, 5/32" (3.8 mm) diameter, optional

- Cambric, optional; 2 yd. (1.85 m) for four chair seats

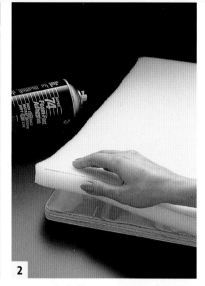
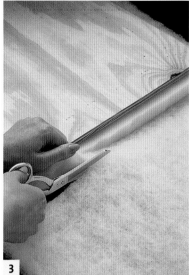

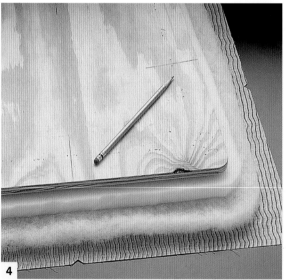
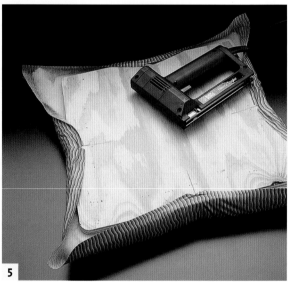

1. REMOVE the screws on the underside of the seat; remove the seat. Strip off the existing outer fabric, using a staple remover or tack lifter. If the foundation is intact, omit steps 2 and 3.

2. APPLY spray adhesive to one side of the foam; affix foam to the top of the seat.

3. PLACE upholstery batting on the table; place the seat, foam side down, over the batting. Wrap batting around the top and sides of the seat. Trim excess batting even with the bottom edge of the seat.

4. MARK the center of each side on the bottom of the seat. Notch the center of each side of the fabric. Place the fabric on the table, wrong side up. Center the seat upside down over the fabric.

5. STAPLE the fabric to the bottom of the seat at the center back, matching the center marks. Stretch the fabric from the back to front; staple at the center front, matching the center marks. Repeat at the center of each side.

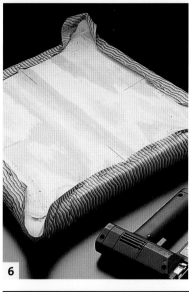

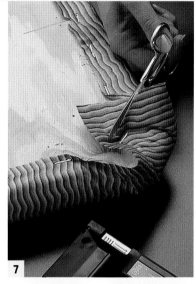

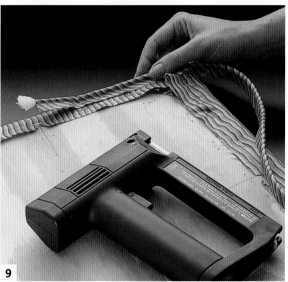

6. APPLY staples to the back of the seat at 1¹/₂" (3.8 cm) intervals, working from the center toward the sides, to within 3" (7.6 cm) of the corners. Pull the fabric taut toward the front of the seat; staple. Repeat for the sides.

7. FOLD the fabric diagonally at the corner; stretch the fabric taut, and staple between the screw hole and the corner. Trim excess fabric diagonally across the corner.

8. MITER fabric at the corner by folding in each side up to the corner; staple in place. Repeat for the remaining corners. Trim excess fabric, exposing screw holes. If welting is not desired, omit step 9. If cambric is not desired, omit step 10.

9. MAKE welting as on page 46, steps 1 to 4. Staple welting around the seat at ³/₄" (1.9 cm) intervals, starting at the back of the seat; align the stitching line of the welting to the edge of the seat. Follow tips on page 48.

10. FOLD under the raw edges of the cambric; staple to the bottom of the seat at 1" (2.5 cm) intervals. Puncture cambric at the screw holes in the chair seat. Screw the upholstered seat to the chair.

CARVED-WOOD FOOTSTOOL

Among the great finds at antique stores are footstools with lovely carved-wood frames. If the frame is still in good condition, the footstool can be restored to like-new condition by replacing the upholstery. Covered with a traditional fabric, such as tapestry or hand-stitched needlepoint, and trimmed with contrasting gimp or decorative nails, the footstool becomes a handsome room accessory. Use gimp that matches the fabric if decorative upholstery nails will be applied over the gimp, or use a matching or contrasting color if the gimp will be used alone as a decorative edging.

The style shown here has a webbed base, originally covered with padding; possibly hair, cotton, or even straw. If the footstool originally had a spring foundation, with the webbing attached to the underside of the frame, you may wish to attach new webbing (page 28) and retie the springs (page 32). For the easiest method of upholstery, however, attach new webbing to the upper side of the frame and pad the top with foam and batting.

YOU WILL NEED

- Webbing and webbing stretcher
- Burlap
- Staple gun and staples, ³/₈" or ¹/₂" (1 or 1.3 cm)
- Foam, 1" (2.5 cm) thick
- Aerosol foam adhesive
- Polyester upholstery batting
- Decorator fabric, such as tapestry fabric or hand-stitched needlepoint
- Gimp trim
- Hot glue gun and glue sticks
- Decorative upholstery nails and upholstery hammer, optional
- Cambric, for dustcover

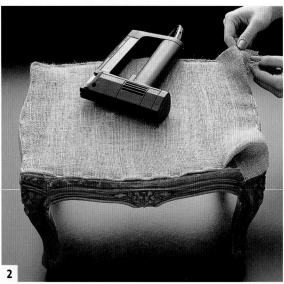

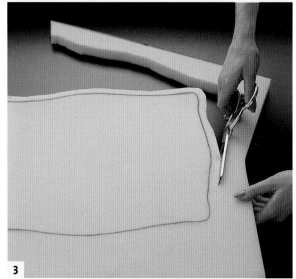

1. Strip all layers of the old fabric, padding, burlap, and webbing from the stool; remove all decorative nails and tacks. Refinish the wood frame, if necessary.

2. Attach webbing to the upper side of the frame as on pages 30 and 31, steps 1 to 6. Cut burlap 3" (7.6 cm) larger than the footstool frame. Fold under the edge of the burlap piece; staple it to the top of the frame, over the webbing, at 1¹/₂" (3.8 cm) intervals, stretching the burlap taut.

3. Place the footstool upside down on the foam; draw an outline of the frame on the foam, using a pencil. Cut the foam ¹/₂" (1.3 cm) beyond the marked lines, using a scissors.

4. Apply aerosol adhesive to the marked side of the foam and to the burlap. Place the footstool upside down on the foam, pressing down so the foam adheres to the burlap. Stand the footstool right side up; press down on the foam.

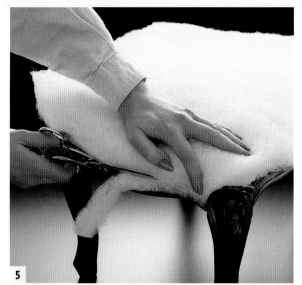

5

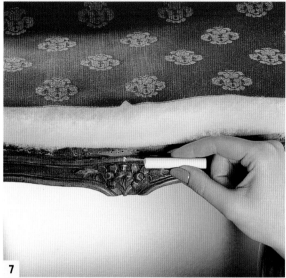

7

6

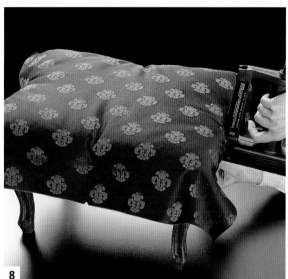

8

5. PLACE a layer of upholstery batting over the foam, wrapping it around the sides of the footstool; trim excess batting above the decorative wood.

6. MEASURE the footstool length and width from the decorative wood on one side, over the foam and batting, to the decorative wood on the opposite side. Add 5" (12.7 cm) to these measurements; cut decorator fabric to this size.

7. NOTCH the center of each side of the fabric; mark the decorative wood on the center of each side of the footstool frame, using chalk.

8. PLACE the fabric, right side up, over the batting. Staple-baste the center of the fabric at the center on the front of the frame, just above the decorative wood, then at the center on the back of the frame, stretching the fabric slightly. Repeat in the other direction, staple-basting fabric at the center of each side.

UPHOLSTERY PROJECTS

79

continued on next page

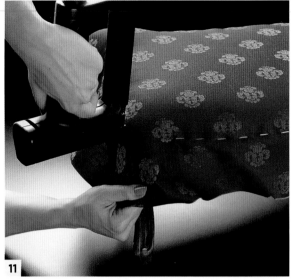

9. REMOVE the center staple from the front of the frame; stretch the fabric taut, and staple again at the center. Working from the center toward one side, apply staples at 1" (2.5 cm) intervals, stretching the fabric taut; stop 3" (7.6 cm) from the corner. Repeat, working from the center toward the opposite side.

10. REPEAT step 9 on the back of the footstool, stretching the fabric taut; then repeat for the sides of the stool.

11. STRETCH the fabric at the corner, dividing excess fullness equally on each side of the corner; insert one staple, centered above the leg, just above the decorative wood.

12. FOLD the fabric as shown, forming an inverted pleat, or "V", at the corner, folding out all excess fabric. Staple in place. Repeat at the remaining corners.

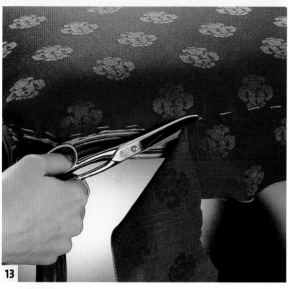

13

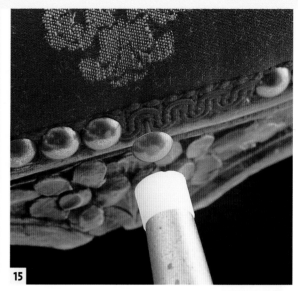

15

14

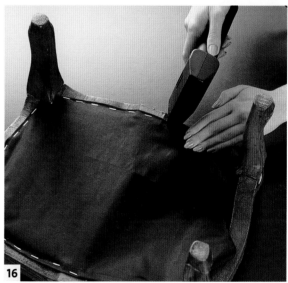

16

13. FINISH stapling each side at 1" (2.5 cm) intervals, up to the corners, stretching the fabric taut. Trim excess fabric on all sides of the footstool, just above the decorative wood.

14. GLUE gimp above the decorative wood, using a hot glue gun, starting at the center of one side; make sure that the raw edges and staples are covered. Fold under 1/2" (1.3 cm) at the ends of the gimp, and butt the folded ends together. Omit step 15 if decorative nails are not being used.

15. TAP the decorative nails into the wood, using an upholstery hammer; center the nails over the gimp. Check the position of each nail before driving it in; if necessary, adjust the vertical or horizontal position by tapping the side of the nail head slightly. Insert the nails head-to-head all around the footstool.

16. CUT cambric 2" (5.1 cm) larger than the bottom of the footstool. Fold under the edges of the cambric; staple the cambric to the bottom of the footstool at 1" (2.5 cm) intervals.

A TWIN BED WITH A PADDED, UPHOLSTERED HEADBOARD MAKES A SMALL BEDROOM COZY AND INVITING.

HEADBOARD

An upholstered headboard is a welcome addition to the bedroom. Padded with foam and batting, this headboard provides comfortable support for reading or watching television. A padded band of gathered fabric outlines the curved top and straight sides of this headboard. Choose upholstery fabric to blend with the bedroom décor. To avoid having to piece the center padded section on larger headboards, choose fabric that can be railroaded (page 17).

You can make an upholstered headboard to fit any size bed. The headboard attaches to the bed frame, so measure the width of the frame and add 2" (5.1 cm) to allow room for drilling bolt holes. For the height, measure from the bottom of the attachment plate on the frame to the desired height above the mattress. The height of the headboard is a matter of personal taste but generally, the smaller the bed, the shorter the headboard should be. For this twin bed, the headboard is 42" (106.7 cm) wide and 36" (91.4 cm) high.

YOU WILL NEED

- Plywood, $1/2$" (1.3 cm) thick
- Saw
- Wood glue
- Coarse-thread sheetrock screws, 1" (2.5 cm) long
- Firm foam, 2" (5.1 cm) thick
- Foam glue
- Polyester batting
- Staple gun and staples, $3/8$" and $1/2$" (1 and 1.3 cm)
- Welt cording
- Upholstery fabric
- Cardboard tacking strip, $1/2$" (1.3 cm) wide
- 3" (7.6 cm) curved needle and #18 nylon thread
- Bolts and nuts for attaching headboard to frame

HOW TO MAKE THE FRAME FOR A HEADBOARD

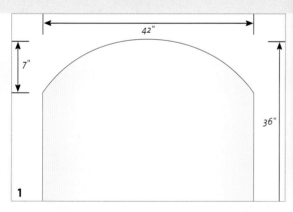

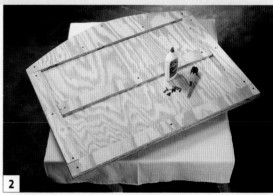

1. CUT a rectangle of $1/2$" (1.3 cm) plywood in the width and height you need, following the guidelines above. Mark a point 7" (17.8 cm) down from the top corner on each side and draw a gentle curve from these points across the top of the board. Check for symmetry, and then saw on the marked line. Cut another rectangle of plywood 8" (20.3 cm) by the headboard width. Shape the upper edge to match the headboard curve. Cut 3" (7.6 cm) support strips of plywood for the bottom, sides, and center.

2. GLUE, then screw the support pieces to the back of the headboard, following the diagram and photo. Take care not to insert screws where you will need to drill bolt holes for attaching the headboard to the bed frame.

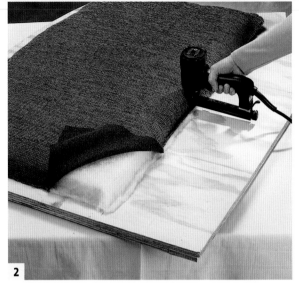

1. MEASURE the height of the frame, box spring, and mattress, and mark a line across the headboard at this distance from the bottom. Draw a line 3" (7.6 cm) from the edge along the sides and top, beginning at the first marked line. This marks the width of the gathered border. Cut a piece of foam to fit the center section of the upper headboard, and glue it in place. Lay a half layer of batting over the foam, and staple it in place.

2. CUT fabric several inches larger than the foam. Mark the center of each side. Also mark the center of each side of the pad-

ded section of the headboard. Place the fabric over the batting, aligning the centers. Pull the fabric evenly and staple it to the frame, starting in the centers and working out toward the corners. Trim off excess fabric.

3. MEASURE the outer edge of the headboard, beginning and ending at the bottom of the padded section. Prepare welting (page 46) slightly longer than this measurement. Cut a 6½" (16.5 cm) strip of fabric one-and-one-half times this length for the gathered border. Stitch the welting to one edge of the border strip, distributing

the fullness evenly. Using ³/8" (1 cm) staples, staple the border strip to the headboard around the padded section with the welting seam 3" (7.6 cm) from the edge. Use a 3" (7.6 cm) strip of cardboard tack strip as a gauge.

4. PLACE the cardboard tack strip over the welting seam allowance with the upper edge even with the stitching line. Staple diagonally through the tack strip, using ½" (1.3 cm) staples.

5. CUT batting into 8" (20.3 cm) strips with enough length to cover the border. Center the batting on the tack strip and staple in place.

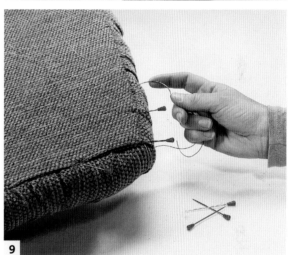

6. Wrap the border strip to the back of the headboard and staple it in place, using $^3/8$" (1 cm) staples. Don't pull the fabric too tightly. It should look full and padded. Staple frequently, distributing the fullness evenly.

7. Cut a piece of fabric large enough to cover the bottom section of the headboard and wrap to the back. Mark the centers of the sides. Place the fabric face-down over the padded section. Staple in place along the bottom of the padded section. Place the cardboard tack strip over the edge, with the upper edge of the strip a distance from the bottom of the headboard equal to the determined depth of the frame, box spring, and mattress (step 1). Staple through the tack strip.

8. Turn down the fabric, wrap it to the back of the headboard, and staple in place, using $^3/8$" (1 cm) staples. This area is unpadded to allow it to fit closely to the frame, box spring, and mattress.

9. Cut a piece of fabric large enough to cover the back of the headboard plus a 1" (2.5 cm) margin all around for turning under. Place the fabric, wrong side up, over the lower edge, and staple in place through the tack strip. Turn under the sides even with the sides of the headboard. Turn the fabric up, turn under the edges, and pin in place. Blindstitch (page 69) the outside back to the headboard, using a 3" (7.6 cm) curved needle and #18 nylon thread.

HOW TO ATTACH THE HEADBOARD

Hold the headboard up to the head of the bed, aligning the lower edge to the lower edge of the attachment plates on the frame. Mark the placement of holes for bolts. Punch holes in the fabric before drilling to prevent catching and tearing the fabric. Secure the headboard to the frame with bolts and nuts.

A SMALL PARSONS BENCH UPHOLSTERED IN GEOMETRIC, SCULPTED CHENILLE FABRIC MAKES A BOLD STATEMENT.
IT ONLY TAKES TWO PIECES OF FABRIC TO COVER THIS CONTEMPORARY FURNITURE PIECE.

PARSONS BENCH

Benches provide extra seating for the living room, family room, or bedroom. This Parsons bench is a contemporary design that is easy to build and upholster. Its finished size is 18" (45.7 cm) high, 15" (38.1 cm) wide, and 29" (73.7 cm) long. This size works well when placed at the foot of a twin-size bed. You can make a longer Parsons bench by lengthening the center section of the frame and widening the legs for extra support.

The wood frame consists of matching, shaped front and back pieces cut from plywood, which are connected by 1 x 3 poplar support boards. To make the bench strong enough to support heavy weight, make the frame front and back from soft maple or oak or double the thickness of the plywood, altering the length of the support boards as necessary.

CUTTING DIRECTIONS

Cut a piece of fabric 27" x 66" (68.6 x 168 cm) for the top of the bench. Cut a piece of fabric 16" x 50" (40.6 x 127 cm) for the underside of the bench.

Cut a piece of burlap 16" x 60" (40.6 x 152.4 cm) for the top of the bench. Cut a piece of burlap 16" x 47" (40.6 x 119 cm) for the underside of the bench.

Cut a piece of 1" (2.5 cm) foam 14$\frac{1}{2}$" x 19" (36.8 x 48.3 cm). Cut another piece of foam 14$\frac{1}{2}$" x 57" (36.8 x 145 cm). Cut a piece of batting 27" x 60" (68.6 x 152.4 cm).

YOU WILL NEED

- Plywood, $\frac{3}{4}$" (1.9 cm) thick

- Saber saw

- 1 x 3 poplar boards

- Wood glue

- 28 coarse-thread sheetrock screws, 2" (5.1 cm) long

- Webbing and webbing stretcher

- Staple gun and staples, $\frac{3}{8}$" and $\frac{1}{2}$" (1 and 1.3 cm)

- Burlap, 40" (101.6 cm) wide, 2 yd. (1.85 m)

- Foam, 1" (2.5 cm) thick, 58" x 24" (147.3 x 61 cm)

- Foam glue

- Polyester batting, 27" (68.6 cm) wide, 2 yd. (1.85 m)

- Upholstery fabric, 2 yd. (1.85 m)

- Upholstery regulator

- Cardboard tack strip, $\frac{1}{2}$" (1.3 cm) wide

- 3" (7.6 cm) curved needle and #18 nylon thread

- Four chair glides

1

Dimensions shown: 17", 4", 29", 13¹/₈", 2³/₄"

2

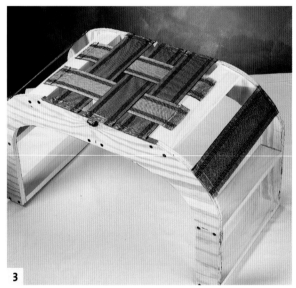

3

1. CUT two pieces of plywood 17" x 29" (43.2 x 73.7 cm) for the bench front and back. Shape the pieces following the graphed pattern, and cut them out with a saber saw. Cut seven poplar boards, each 13¹/₄" (33.7 cm) long.

2. APPLY wood glue to one end of one support board, and align it to the bottom of a leg on the bench front. Secure it by inserting two screws. Repeat for the other leg. Then attach a support 8¹/₂" (21.6 cm) from the bottom on each leg. At the top of the bench, attach two supports parallel to and flush with the upper edge 6¹/₄" (15.9 cm) from each side

of center. Attach the final support parallel to and flush with the underside of the seat at the center. Turn the frame over and secure the bench back to the supports in the same way. Allow the glue to dry.

3. ATTACH three webbing strips from front to back across the top of the bench, evenly spaced between the supports, following the directions on pages 30 to 31. Also attach a webbing strip at each outer top curve. Weave two webbing strips through the top three strips in the opposite direction, and secure them to the top supports.

4

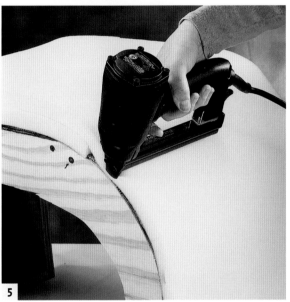

5

6

4. PLACE the large piece of burlap over the frame. Stretch the burlap taut side to side and end to end, and staple it to the outer edge of the frame using ³/8" (1 cm) staples. Turn back the edge all around and staple again.

5. GLUE the small piece of foam to the top center of the burlap. Glue the center of the large foam piece over the small foam piece. Staple the foam to the outer edge of the frame over the curves, down the sides, and across the bottom of the legs.

6. WRAP the batting over the frame and staple in place along the lower edges. Trim off excess batting.

continued on next page

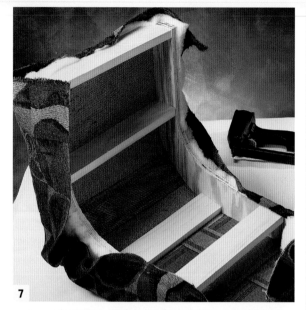

7. Mark the centers of the sides of the top fabric. Mark the center of the front and back on the underside of the bench; also mark the centers of the underside of both legs. Stretch the fabric over the top of the bench and wrap it evenly to the underside, aligning center marks. Staple the centers and for about 3" (7.6 cm) from each side of center. Then stretch the fabric to the ends of the legs and wrap it to the underside, aligning center marks. Staple about 3" (7.6 cm) at the center of each leg.

8. Check to make sure the fabric is evenly stretched. Wrap fabric over the leg edges up to the curve, and staple. Miter the bottom corners and staple. Using a regulator, fold the fabric into pleats at the curves and staple in place. The pleats should be evenly

spaced about 1¹/₂" (3.8 cm) apart at the underside of the frame, fanning wider at the top, with all folds turned away from center. Trim fabric even with the inner edge of the frame.

9. Place the underside fabric, facedown, along one edge of the underside and staple in place, using ³/₈" (1 cm) staples. Place the tack strip over the fabric even with the outer edge of the bench and staple, using ¹/₂" (1.3 cm) staples.

10

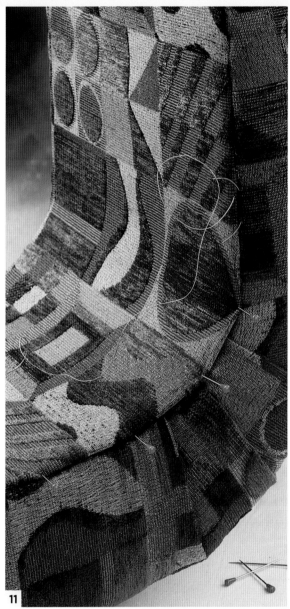

11

10. STAPLE the remaining burlap piece over the underside of the frame. On the side opposite the tack strip, turn back the edge and staple again.

11. TURN the fabric over the burlap and stretch it to the other side. Turn under the edge and pin in place. Fold under and miter fabric on the underside of each leg, and staple in place. Blindstitch (page 69) the pinned edge, using a 3"(7.6 cm) curved needle and #18 nylon thread. Attach two glides to the underside of each leg.

THIS SIDE CHAIR HAS A DECORATIVE FRAME AROUND THE INSET CHAIR BACK AND AT THE LOWER EDGE OF THE BOXED SEAT. DOUBLE WELTING TRIMS THE SEAT, BACK, AND ARMS.

SIDE CHAIRS

Small side chairs, often referred to as pull-up chairs, provide convenient extra seating when entertaining guests. The easy boxed-seat upholstery techniques on pages 94 to 99 can be used for a variety of side chair styles. These chairs may originally have padded boxed seats and inset backs, often framed with exposed decorative wood. Similar chairs may have pullover-style seats or loose boxed cushions. Chairs that originally had spring foundation seats can also be reupholstered using this easier method, if desired.

Before reupholstering, strip all layers of old fabric, padding, and burlap, and remove old webbing and any springs from the seat. Back webbing that is still in good condition and taut need not be replaced, unless the chair style has exposed wood with only a front tacking rail. Webbing must then be removed in order to replace the fabric that faces the back of the chair. Refurbish the wood frame, if necessary.

CUTTING DIRECTIONS

For the seat of the chair, cut a piece of burlap 3" (7.6 cm) larger than the chair frame. Cut cambric 2" (5.1 cm) larger than the bottom of the chair. Cut the fabric and the foam for the seat top as on page 94, step 2.

Cut the length of the boxing strip equal to the distance around the chair frame plus 2" (5.1 cm) overlap; if it is necessary to seam the boxing strip, add extra for seam allowances. For a chair with an exposed decorative seat frame, cut the width of the boxing strip equal to the foam thickness plus the distance from the top of the frame to the decorative wood plus 1¹/₂" (3.8 cm). For a chair without a decorative seat frame, cut the width of the boxing strip equal to the foam thickness plus the height of the frame plus 1¹/₂" (3.8 cm); the boxing strip wraps around the bottom of the frame.

For the welting in the boxing seam, cut bias fabric strips, 1¹/₂" (3.8 cm) wide; the combined length of the strips is equal to the distance around the chair frame plus extra for seam allowances. For a chair with a decorative seat frame, also cut bias fabric strips, 3" (7.6 cm) wide, if double welting is to be used for the trim around the seat frame.

For the chair back, cut one rectangle of burlap, 5" (12.7 cm) larger than the frame opening. Cut two rectangles of fabric, 5" (12.7 cm) larger than the frame opening; these are to be used for the outside back and inside back pieces. Cut two or three layers of batting to the same size as the opening. If double welting is to be used, cut bias fabric strips, 3" (7.6 cm) wide.

For the chair arms, cut one rectangle of fabric, 4" (10.2 cm) larger than the area to be padded on the arm. Cut the batting to the size of the area to be padded. If double welting is to be used, cut bias fabric strips, 3" (7.6 cm) wide.

SIDE CHAIR (ABOVE) IS UPHOLSTERED WITH A BOXED SEAT THAT WRAPS UNDER THE CHAIR FRAME. THE INSET CHAIR BACK IS TRIMMED WITH DOUBLE WELTING.

YOU WILL NEED

- Muslin

- Upholstery fabric, 2 yd. (1.85 m) for most side chairs

- Foam, 3" or 4" (7.6 or 10.2 cm) thick

- Webbing and webbing stretcher

- Burlap

- Foam adhesive

- Welt cording, ⁵/₃₂" (3.8 mm) diameter

- Polyester or cotton upholstery batting, 27" (68.6 cm) wide, 2 yd. (1.85 m)

- Staple gun and staples, ³/₈" or ¹/₂" (1 or 1.3 cm)

- Braid trim, such as gimp, optional

- Hot glue gun and glue sticks, or white craft glue

- Cambric, for dustcover, 1 yd. (0.92 m)

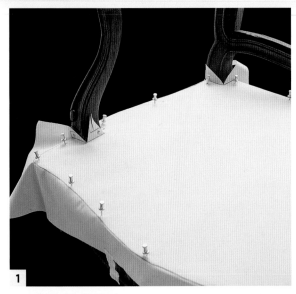

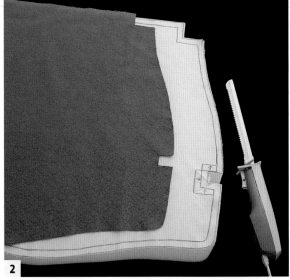

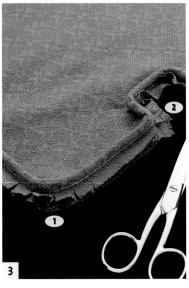

1. MARK a muslin pattern by placing muslin on the frame, securing it with push pins. Mark muslin at the edges of the frame; draw around chair arms. For arms that slope out or back, redraw a line ½" (1.3 cm) from the original line so the tip of the foam will fit around the arm.

2. REMOVE muslin; add ½" (1.3 cm) seam allowances on all sides. Cut the fabric for the seat top, following the pattern; cut the foam to the same size for a firm, tight fit. Apply webbing (page 28) to the chair frame; apply burlap as on page 78, step 2. Affix foam over the burlap, using spray adhesive.

3. MAKE welting and attach it to the right side of the seat top, as on page 46, steps 1 to 6. Clip seam allowances of the welting at ½" (1.3 cm) intervals on rounded corners (1) or make one diagonal clip at the square corners (2).

4. FOLD back 1" (2.5 cm) at the end of the boxing strip; place the strip on the seat top, right sides together, with the fold at the center back. Stitch a seam, crowding the cording; clip the corners as in step 3. At the end of the seam, overlap the ends of the boxing strip.

5. COVER the top and sides of the foam with upholstery batting, cutting the batting around the arm posts; trim away excess batting at the corners. For a chair with a decorative seat frame, trim batting above the decorative wood.

HOW TO UPHOLSTER THE SEAT OF A CHAIR WITH SIDE ARM POSTS

1

2

3

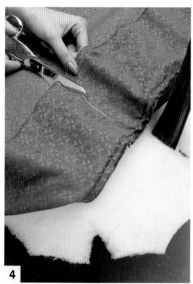

4

5

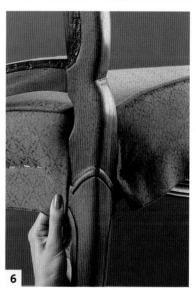

6

Chair with decorative frame

1. PLACE the seat cover over the batting; staple-baste the boxing strip to the frame at the center front, just above the decorative wood. Repeat at the center back.

2. SMOOTH the top of the seat cover from side to side; fold back the boxing strip at the arm post. Mark a line for a Y-cut (page 69) from the raw edge of the boxing strip to within 2" (5.1 cm) of the seam, aligning the mark to the center of the arm post; cut on the marked line.

3. PULL the fabric down around the arm post. Repeat for the opposite arm post.

4. REMOVE staple at the center back. At back corner, fold back the boxing strip diagonally, as for the chair with front arm posts on page 97, step 1. Mark a line from the raw edge to within 2" (5.1 cm) of the seam, aligning the mark to the center of the back post; cut on the marked line. Repeat at the opposite back post. Pull the boxing strip down at the back and side of the chair frame.

5. FOLD under fabric at the side of the chair, with the fold along the back post; staple the boxing strip to the chair frame at the fold.

6. REPEAT step 5 for the opposite side of the chair. On the back of the chair, staple boxing strip to the frame, working from the center toward the sides. At back posts, fold under and staple the fabric as in step 5.

continued on next page

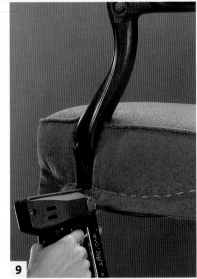

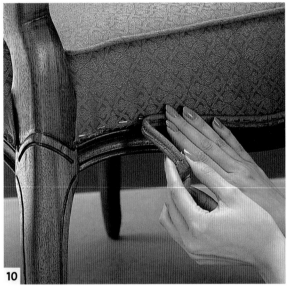

7. PULL the fabric taut toward the front of the chair; staple boxing strip to the front of the frame, working from the center toward the sides of the chair.

8. FOLD under fabric along the front of the arm post as in step 5; staple boxing strip in front of the arm post to the frame.

9. FOLD under fabric on the side of chair along the back of the arm post; staple boxing strip to the side of the frame. Repeat for the opposite side of the chair.

10. TRIM excess fabric on all sides of the chair, just above the decorative wood. Glue double welting (page 49) or gimp above the decorative wood, using hot glue or craft glue, making sure the raw edges and staples are covered. Butt the raw edges of double welting; or remove cording at the ends and fold under the edges. For gimp, fold under the ends.

11. FOLD under the edges of the cambric; stable to the bottom of the chair at 1" (2.5 cm) intervals.

Chair without decorative frame

1. FOLLOW steps 1 to 7 on pages 94 to 96, except pull the lower edge of the boxing strip under the frame, and staple to the bottom of the frame. Cut fabric at the front leg, from lower edge up to point where the leg and the bottom of frame meet; finish stapling boxing strip on the front of the chair frame up to the leg.

2. CUT fabric at the side of the chair, from lower edge up to point where the leg and bottom of the frame meet. At the corner, trim excess fabric, allowing $3/4$" (1.9 cm) to fold under. Fold under fabric at the front leg. Complete the boxed seat as in steps 8 and 9, opposite, stapling the lower edge to the bottom of the frame. Apply cambric as in step 11.

HOW TO UPHOLSTER THE SEAT OF A CHAIR WITH FRONT ARM POSTS

Chair with decorative frame

1. FOLLOW step 1 on page 95. Smooth the top of the seat cover from side to side; align welting seams around the front arm posts. Fold back the boxing strip diagonally at the arm post. Mark a line from the raw edge to within 2" (5.1 cm) of the seam, aligning mark to the center of the arm post; cut on the marked line.

2. PULL the fabric down around the arm post. Repeat for the opposite arm post. Follow steps 4 to 7 on pages 95 and 96. On the front of the chair, fold under and staple the fabric at the arm post as in step 5. Complete the seat as in steps 9 to 11, opposite.

Chair without decorative frame

FOLLOW steps 1 and 2, left, except pull the lower edge of the boxing strip around to the bottom of the chair frame, and staple to the bottom of the frame.

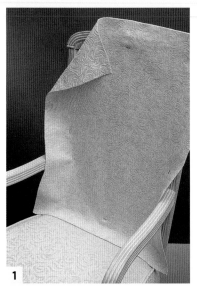

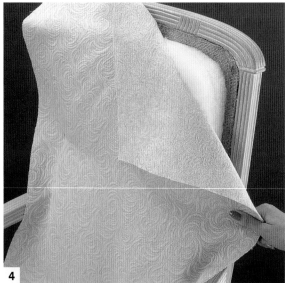

Tacking rail on inside back

1. Apply the fabric rectangle for the outside back, with right side toward the back of the chair, staple-basting fabric at the center top to the tacking rail on the inside back of the frame, ¼" (6 mm) from the molding. Repeat at the center bottom and the center of each side.

2. Staple the fabric from the center bottom, up to the beginning of the curve at the rounded corners or up to 3" (7.6 cm) from the square corners. Staple fabric at the top, stretching the fabric taut; repeat at each side. Staple fabric at the corners. Trim excess fabric next to the staples. Place one layer of batting over the fabric.

3. Apply the webbing strips as on page 31, stapling into the tacking rail; webbing strips do not have to be folded over. Staple burlap over the webbing; trim excess.

4. Place two layers of batting over the burlap. Place the fabric rectangle for the inside back, right side up, over the batting; staple. Trim the excess fabric, and apply double welting or gimp as on page 98, step 10.

Tacking rails on the inside and outside back (bottom)

Follow steps 3 and 4, left and above. From the back of the chair, apply the fabric rectangle for the outside back, right side out, stapling into the tacking rail on the outside back of the frame. Trim excess fabric, and apply the double welting or gimp as on page 96, step 10.

HOW TO UPHOLSTER THE CHAIR ARMS

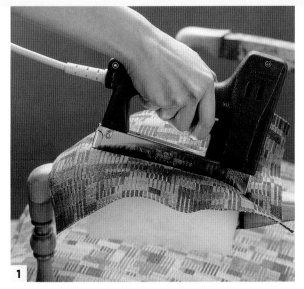

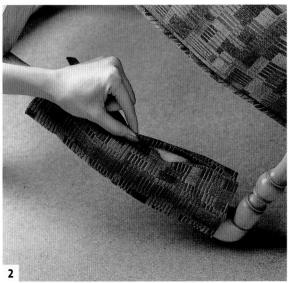

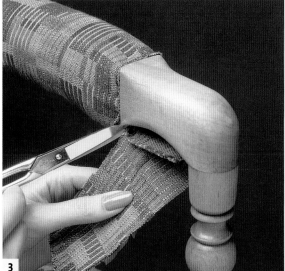

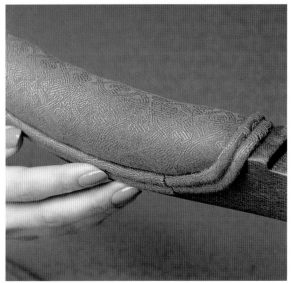

Wrapped arm pad

1. PLACE two or three layers of batting on top of the arm. Place fabric right side up over the batting; staple at the back of the arm.

2. STRETCH to the front of the arm; staple. Pull fabric around the arm; staple to the bottom of the arm. On the opposite side, pull fabric around the arm, folding under the edge; staple.

3. FINISH stapling along the back and front of the arm. Trim excess fabric. Glue the double welting or gimp as on page 96, step 10.

Oval arm pad (bottom)

PLACE two or three layers of batting on top of the arm. Place fabric right side up over the batting. Secure the fabric as for the chair back, steps 1 and 2, opposite. Trim excess fabric, and apply the double welting or gimp as on page 96, step 10; butt ends of the double welting, or fold under ends of the gimp.

UPHOLSTERED IN BLUE TWEED CHENILLE, THESE PARSONS CHAIRS ARE TRANSITIONAL PIECES THAT WOULD FIT EQUALLY WELL WITH SEVERAL FURNITURE STYLES, INCLUDING TRADITIONAL, ARTS AND CRAFTS, ART NOUVEAU, OR MISSION.

PARSONS CHAIR

Parsons chairs are very versatile. They easily blend with other furniture styles. Like a chameleon, a Parsons chair takes on the style of the fabric used to cover it. If your dining room furniture is traditional in style, a Parsons chair covered in brocade or velvet enhances the setting. If you want more contemporary Parsons chairs, cover them with bold geometric print fabric or microfiber suede. Parsons chairs are usually used in the dining room, but they also fit nicely as side chairs in the living room.

Parsons chairs are distinguished by their straight or slightly arched, solid backs that adjoin padded seats with straight legs—all entirely covered with fabric. The chair back can be straight, camelback, or scrolled (rolled), like the chair shown here. Also like this Parsons chair, they are usually armless, though some styles have arms that are upholstered, or upholstered scrolled. For those styles, refer to the directions on page 99 for upholstering the arms.

Measure all the chair parts (page 20) and record the measurements. Determine the cut sizes of all the parts and graph the fabric layout (page 22). Mark the right side of the fabric, using chalk and following the graphed layout; label each piece. Cut out the pieces. Mark the center front and back of the seat and the center top and bottom of the back pieces. Cut cambric 2" (5.1 cm) larger than the bottom of the chair. Strip the chair, following the guidelines on page 25. Mark the center front and back on the seat and chair back. Take careful notes, and adjust the upholstery steps when necessary.

YOU WILL NEED

- Polyester batting, 4 yd. (3.7 m) per chair
- Upholstery fabric, approximately $2^3/_4$ yd. (2.55 m) per chair
- Staple gun and staples, $3/_8$" and $1/_2$" (1 and 1.3 cm)
- Foam, 1" (2.5 cm) thick
- Four small plastic trash-can liners
- Welt cording, $5/_{32}$" (3.8 mm) diameter, 2 yd. (1.85 m)
- Cardboard tack strip, 2 yd. (1.85 m)
- Burlap
- 3" (7.6 cm) curved needle and #18 nylon thread
- Cambric, for dustcover
- Four chair glides

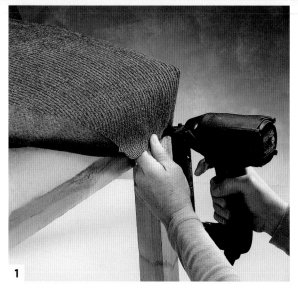

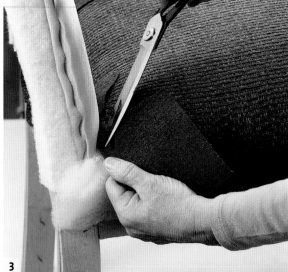

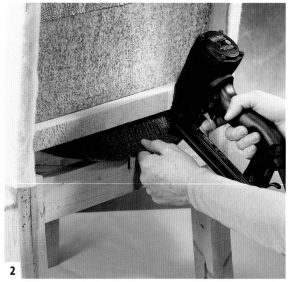

1. REPLACE or supplement the batting over the seat foam, as necessary. Place the seat fabric, wrong side up, over the seat and pin it to fit at the corners. Mark the corner stitching lines with chalk. Stitch the corners and trim off excess fabric. Replace the seat cover, right side up. Pull the seat cover down at the corners and staple it in place, using 3/8" (1 cm) staples.

2. PULL the seat cover through to the back. Staple the cover in place at the center back and about 4" (10.2 cm) out to each side of the center.

3. SMOOTH the top of the seat cover from side to side. Fold back the fabric at one back post, and mark a line for a Y-cut (page 69), aligning the mark to the center of the post; cut on the marked line. Pull the fabric down around the back post, and staple in place. Repeat for the other side. Finish stapling the seat cover in place.

4. REPLACE or supplement the foam and batting on the inside back, as necessary. Place the fabric over the inside back. Pull it through to the back at the bottom and staple it in place, working from the center out.

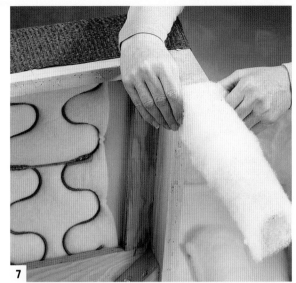

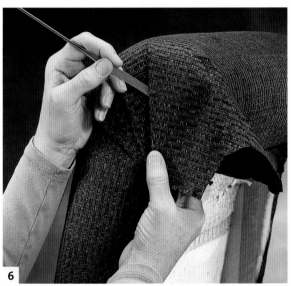

5. SMOOTH the inside back fabric up from the bottom over the top of the chair back. Matching the center of the fabric to the center of the chair back, staple the fabric in place at the center and about 4" (10.2 cm) out to each side of the center. Make Y-cuts (as in step 3) to fit the fabric around the posts at the bottom of the inside back.

6. SMOOTH the inside back cover from side to side, wrapping it around to the back. Staple the fabric to the back of the chair. Using a regulator, form pleats in the fabric to conform it to the top curve of the back; staple the pleats in place. Finish stapling the inside back in place. Trim off excess fabric.

7. MEASURE the circumference and length of each chair leg. Cut four pieces of polyester batting 1" (2.5 cm) wider and the same length as the measurements. Stitch the batting into tubes, using 1/2" (1.3 cm) seams; turn them right side out. Slide a batting tube onto each leg and staple it in place at the top and bottom.

8. SLIDE a small plastic trash-can liner over each leg. Wrap the leg fabric around the leg, wrong side out, and pin in place. Mark the seam line with chalk. Remove the pins and sew the seam; trim off excess fabric. Turn the leg tube right side out and slide it onto the chair leg over the plastic, aligning the seam to the inside corner. Clip the upper edge of the leg tube at the four corners and staple it in place. Repeat for the other legs.

continued on next page

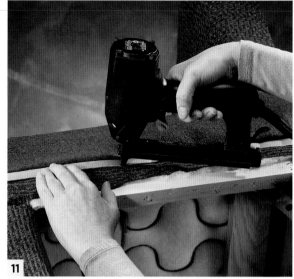

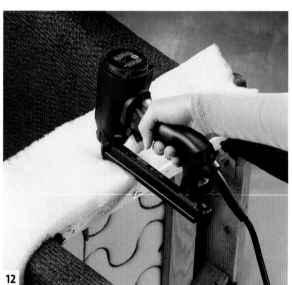

9. SMOOTH the leg fabric down over the bottom of the leg. Trim excess fabric and miter the folds; staple it in place.

10. PREPARE welting as on page 46. Sew the welting to the upper edge of the chair band. Place the band, wrong side up, over the sides and front of the chair. The stitching line of the welting should align to the top of the wood seat. Staple in place along the welting seam allowance. Use a piece of cardboard tack strip as a gauge.

11. PLACE the cardboard tack strip over the welting seam allowance, with the upper edge even with the stitching line. Staple diagonally through the tack strip.

12. CUT a strip of batting the length of the band and twice the finished height of the band. Lay the batting over the band with the center of the batting over the welting seam line. Staple horizontally along the upper edge of the tack strip. Be sure to staple right at the corners.

13

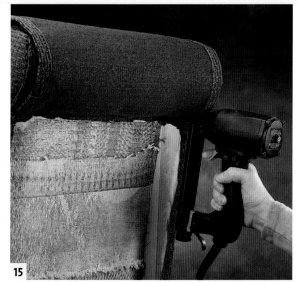

15

14

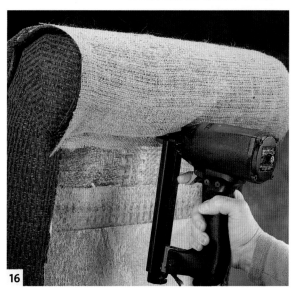

16

13. TURN the band down and pull it snugly to the underside of the frame. Staple, beginning at the center front, using $3/8$" (1 cm) staples. Stop 1" (2.5 cm) from each side of each leg. Angle-cut from the leg to the upper corner on both sides of each leg.

14. TURN under the fabric over the legs. Finish stapling the band to the underside of the frame at the sides and front. Wrap the band to the chair back, folding under the lower edge across the leg, and staple. Trim off excess fabric.

15. PLACE the outside back fabric piece, wrong side up, over the chair back, and staple the upper edge in place. Turn under the sides even with the sides of the chair back.

16. CUT a piece of burlap slightly larger than the outside chair back. Place the burlap over the chair back fabric. Staple along the upper edge.

continued on next page

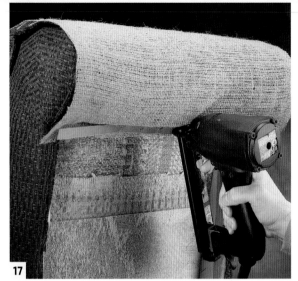

17

19

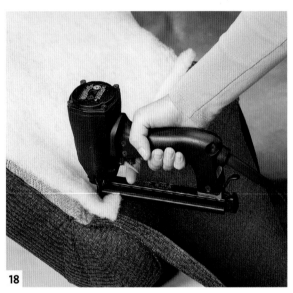

18

20

17. Cut a piece of cardboard tack strip the width of the outside back. Place the tack strip over the upper edge of the burlap and outside back. Staple in place using ¹/₂" (1.3 cm) staples.

18. Turn down the burlap. Turn under the lower edge and staple to the bottom of the outside back. Turn under the sides and staple in place. Cut a piece of batting the same width as the chair back and slightly longer than the back. Separate the batting to use only a half layer. Place the half layer of batting over the burlap on the chair back with the upper edge of the batting extending 1" (2.5 cm) above the tack strip. Staple the batting in place along the tack strip. Also staple the batting to the bottom of the frame and three times along each side.

19. Turn down the outside back fabric over the batting. Pull the lower edge to the underside of the frame and staple at the center and about 4" (10.2 cm) out to each side of the center. Turn under the fabric at the sides of the outside back even with the edges of the chair, and pin them in place to within 2" (5.1 cm) of the leg corners.

20. Angle-cut the lower edge of the outside back from about the center of the leg to the inner corner of the leg on both sides. Fold under the fabric across the legs and pin in place. Finish stapling the lower edge to the underside of the frame.

21. BLINDSTITCH (page 69) the outside back to the chair along the sides, using a 3" (7.6 cm) curved needle and #18 nylon thread.

22. ATTACH cambric to the underside of the frame as on page 96, step 11.

23. INSTALL a glide to the center bottom of each leg. If the chair will go on hardwood or tile, attach felt pads to the glides.

STORAGE OTTOMAN

A storage ottoman is a versatile, multifunctional furniture piece. It's a comfortable place to rest your feet and a handy container for storing books, magazines, DVDs, toys, or your latest knitting project. The wooden frame is easy to build, and you can cover it in any type of upholstery fabric to suit the décor of the room.

To construct the frame, you first build a plywood cube and then saw the top off using a table saw with a fence for accuracy. It is very important to place screws exactly as directed so they will be out of the way of the saw blade. In the directions that follow, glides are attached to the bottom of the ottoman. You can attach casters, if you prefer, but be sure to take into account the additional height and adjust the height of the frame as necessary.

CUTTING DIRECTIONS

Cut $3/4$" (1.9 cm) plywood into the following pieces: two 13" x 16" (33 x 40.6 cm) and two 13" x 14" (33 x 35.6 cm) for the frame sides and two 14" x $17^{1}/2$" (35.6 x 44.5 cm) for the top and bottom. Cut two pieces of $1/8$" (3 mm) plywood or MDF 12" x $15^{1}/2$" (30.5 x 39.4 cm) for the inside top and bottom inserts.

Cut a rectangle of 1" (2.5 cm) foam $14^{1}/4$" x $18^{1}/4$" (36.2 x 46.4 cm). Cut a 23" x 27" (58.4 x 68.6 cm) piece of batting for the lid and a 10" x $32^{1}/2$" (25.4 x 82.6 cm) piece of batting for the bottom.

Cut a $33^{1}/2$" x 37" (85.1 x 94 cm) piece of fabric to cover the outside of the lid. Cut a $23^{1}/2$" x $32^{1}/2$" (59.7 x 82.6 cm) piece of fabric to cover the outside and inside of the bottom. Cut two pieces of fabric 14" x $17^{1}/2$" (35.6 x 44.5 cm) to cover the inside top and bottom inserts.

Cut cambric $19^{1}/2$" x 16" (49.5 x 40.6 cm).

Label all the pieces.

YOU WILL NEED

- Plywood, $3/4$" (1.9 cm) thick
- Saw
- Plywood or MDF, $1/8$" (3 mm) thick
- Wood glue
- Coarse-thread wood screws, 2" (5.1 cm) long
- Table saw with a fence
- Firm foam, 1" (2.5 cm) thick
- Polyester batting, 2 yd. (1.85 m)
- Upholstery fabric, approximately 2 yd. (1.85 m)
- Staple gun and staples, $3/8$" (1 cm) and $1/4$" (6 mm)
- Short finishing nails
- Curved needle and #18 thread
- Cambric, for dustcover
- Four chair glides
- Two continuous hinges
- Friction lid support

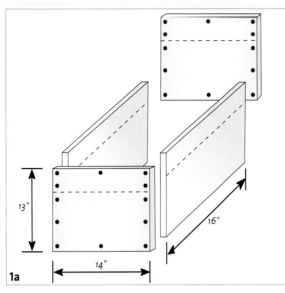

1a

2

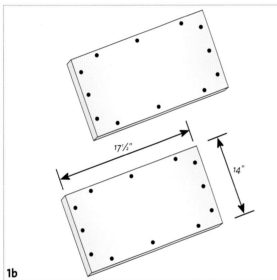

1b

3

1. Assemble the frame following the diagram. Apply wood glue along the narrow edges before inserting the screws. Be sure to insert screws in the locations indicated. The assembled frame should be 17¹/₂" x 14" x 14¹/₂" high (44.5 x 35.6 x 36.8 cm). Saw the frame into two pieces 3³/₄" (9.5 cm) from the top, using a table saw with a fence.

2. Center the foam on top of the box lid and glue it in place. Lay the lid batting on the work surface. Place the lid upside down in the center of the batting. Stretch the batting up around the frame and staple it close to the outside of the lid along the edge. Trim off excess batting even with the lid edge. Pleat the batting at the corners and trim out some of the excess batting. Mark the centers of the lid sides on the underside of the lid.

3. Lay the lid fabric facedown on the work surface. Mark the centers of the sides. Place the lid upside down in the center of the fabric. Stretch the fabric evenly around the four sides, slightly compressing the foam. Staple the fabric to the underside of the lid at the centers of the sides, about ¹/₄" (6 mm) from the frame sides. Working out from the center of the short sides first, stretch and staple the fabric in place to the corners. Wrap the fabric over the corners onto the long side, and staple about ¹/₂" (1.3 cm) from the corner up the side and again on the narrow edge.

4

6

5

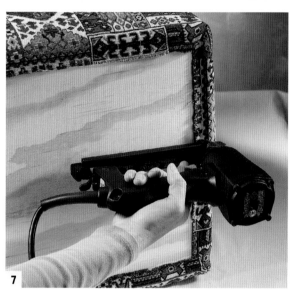

7

4. WORKING out from the center of one long side, stretch and staple the fabric in place. At the corner, pleat out excess fabric so the fold will align to the edge. Trim out some excess fabric. Refold the pleat and pin in place on the edge. Then fold the fabric down the inside of the corner and staple in place. Remove the pin. Repeat at each corner until the lid is covered.

5. CENTER the lid insert on the wrong side of the insert fabric. Wrap the fabric to the back of the board and staple in place with short staples. Push the lid insert into the lid to cover the raw edges and staples. If the lid doesn't fit snugly, secure it with short finishing nails. Manipulate the fabric over the nail heads to hide them.

6. WRAP the lower part of the ottoman with batting. Staple it in place near the upper edge. Stretch it to the bottom and staple it in place along the lower edge. Trim off excess batting.

7. STITCH the two short ends of the bottom fabric right sides together with a $1/2$" (1.3 cm) seam. Turn the cover right side out and slide it onto the ottoman from the top. Wrap about $3/4$" (1.9 cm) to the underside. Staple the fabric to the underside of the frame, mitering the corners.

continued on next page

8. STRETCH the fabric over the upper edge and down to the inside bottom. Staple the fabric to the inside bottom at the centers of the sides, about 1/4" (6 mm) from the frame sides; then work toward the corners. Miter the fabric across the top of each corner, and pin it in place. Pleat out excess fabric so the fold aligns to the corner. Finish stapling.

9. THREAD a curved needle with #18 hand-sewing thread. Blindstitch (page 69) the corner folds in place. Cover the bottom insert with fabric and push it in place as in step 5.

10. TURN under the edges of the cambric and staple it to the underside of the ottoman. Attach a glide to the underside of the ottoman about 1 1/2" (3.8 cm) from each corner.

11. INSTALL continuous hinges along the back of the lid. Install a friction lid support to one side, following the manufacturer's directions.

11

ATTACHED-CUSHION OTTOMAN

This ottoman style has a separate cushion, which appears to be free but is actually attached to the otto-man base by a hidden seam. The cushion may be designed as a boxed cushion with or without welting, or as a welted knife-edge cushion.

The design features of the ottoman, often patterned after a matching chair, can vary in several ways. There may be a skirt (page 63), or it may have decorative legs. On some unskirted ottomans, the nosing, or base sides, are padded and there may be a welted band added around the lower edge.

Much of the outer cover is sewn together before it is attached to the ottoman. Take careful measure-ments of all the pieces before stripping, as accuracy will be crucial in constructing the new outer cover.

Cutting Directions

Measure the ottoman (page 20) and graph the fabric layout (page 22), according to the measurements and the allowances listed opposite. Mark the right side of the fabric, using chalk and label each piece. Cut out the pieces. Cut cambric 2" (5.1 cm) larger than the bottom of the ottoman.

For an ottoman with a boxed cushion, follow the cutting directions on page 50 for a boxed cushion that will be sewn closed. For an ottoman with a knife-edge cushion, follow the cutting directions on page 58 for a cushion that will be exposed on all four sides.

SKIRTED OTTOMAN WITH ATTACHED BOX CUSHION MATCHES THE WING CHAIR IN DESIGN AND PATTERN PLACEMENT. THE SKIRT STYLE WAS CHANGED IN REUPHOLSTERY TO GIVE THE FURNITURE AN UPDATED LOOK.

Cut a piece of fabric for each side and end panel of the nosing 1" (2.5 cm) wider than the measured width before stripping. For a skirted ottoman, the cut length of each nosing piece is 5½" (14 cm) longer than the height of the ottoman from the lower edge to the upper edge. For an ottoman with a lower band, the cut length of each nosing piece is 5½" (14 cm) longer than the distance from the top of the band to the upper edge.

If the ottoman has a skirt, follow the cutting directions on page 63 for the desired skirt style.

If the ottoman has a lower band, cut pieces for the band 2½" (6.4 cm) longer and 1" (2.5 cm) wider than the measurements of the band pieces before stripping.

Cut fabric strips for the welting (page 45), with the total length equal to the total length of the welting, measured before stripping, plus additional length for seaming strips, joining ends, and inconspicuously positioning seams.

YOU WILL NEED

- Graph paper
- Polyester batting or cotton batting
- Foam
- Foam spray adhesive
- Polyester batting, for replacing cushion insert, if necessary
- Cambric, for dustcover
- 3" (7.6 cm) curved needle and heavy thread
- Staple gun and staples, ⅜" (1 cm)
- Tack strip

OTTOMAN WITH WELTED BAND WAS REUPHOLSTERED WITH A KNIFE-EDGE CUSHION AND GIVEN CONTEMPORARY WOODEN BUN FEET.

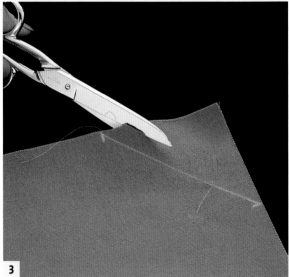

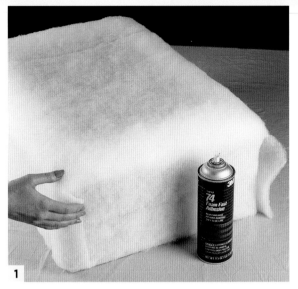

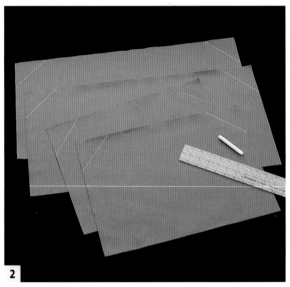

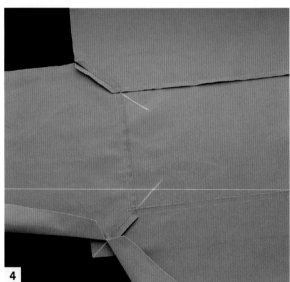

1. STRIP the ottoman (page 25); check the foundation for stability. Make any necessary frame repairs (page 26); replace the webbing (page 28) and retie the springs (page 32), if necessary. Replace or supplement the ottoman padding with polyester or cotton batting as necessary.

2. MARK points 3¹/₂" (8.9 cm) from top corners on the sides and upper edges of the nosing pieces. Draw seam lines on the wrong side of the nosing pieces, connecting marked points.

3. PIN the nosing pieces, right sides together, forming a continuous circle; stitch along the marked lines, stopping 1¹/₂" (3.8 cm) from the side edges. Trim seam allowances to ¹/₂" (1.3 cm); press open.

4. MARK lines at 45 degree angles from the corners, on the right side of the cushion bottom, using chalk and a straightedge. Place the nosing over the cushion bottom, right sides together, aligning the seams to marked diagonal lines; pin. Stitch ¹/₂" (1.3 cm) from inner edges of the nosing.

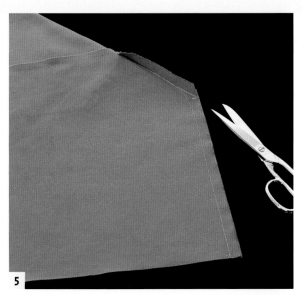

5

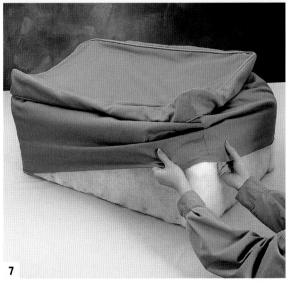

7

6

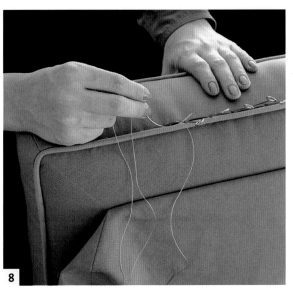

8

5. STITCH ¹/₂" (1.3 cm) side seams of the nosing, overlapping the angled stitching lines at the upper edges; round the corners slightly. Trim as necessary. Press the seams open.

6. COMPLETE the cushion cover as on page 55, steps 1 to 4, for a boxed cushion or page 59, steps 1 and 2, for a knife-edge cushion; tuck the nosing inside the cushion cover to keep it free of the stitches. Turn the cover right side out.

7. SMOOTH the cover in place over the ottoman. Check the fit; check for symmetry. Add polyester batting for padding, if necessary. Remove the cover and adjust the seams, if necessary.

8. PREPARE and insert the cushion as on pages 59 to 61.

continued on next page

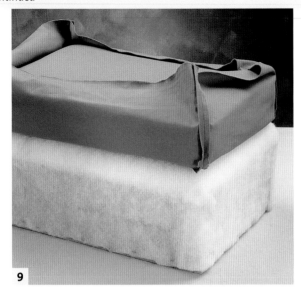

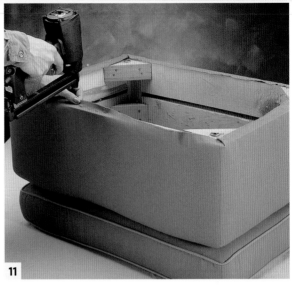

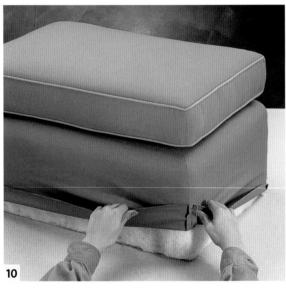

9. FLIP the nosing up, inside out, over the cushion; place the cushion on the ottoman base.

10. PULL the nosing down over the corners, one at a time, holding the padding in place. The corner seams should fit snugly over the base corners.

11. PULL the nosing down taut over the base; wrap to the underside, and staple or tack securely at the centers of the sides. Then staple or tack the nosing securely to the underside of the base, working from the centers toward the sides.

12. FOLD under the edges of the cambric dustcover; staple to the bottom of the ottoman at 1" (2.5 cm) intervals. Make and attach a skirt (page 63), if desired.

HOW TO UPHOLSTER AN OTTOMAN WITH A WELTED BAND

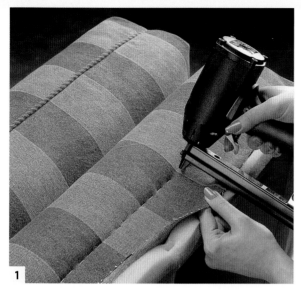

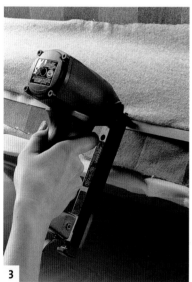

1. FOLLOW steps 1 to 8 on pages 116 and 117. Pull the nosing down snugly over the base; staple-baste near the lower edge. Staple securely just below the placement line for the lower band, stapling first at centers of the sides and then working toward the corners.

2. STITCH the band pieces together into a continuous circle, stitching ½" (1.3 cm) seams. Prepare welting as on page 64, steps 5 to 7. Sew the welting to the upper edge of the band strip, matching pin marks to the seams and easing the band to fit.

3. MARK the base with chalk at the desired height of the welt seam, measuring up from the floor. Staple the band to the ottoman base as for the skirt on page 65, steps 11 and 12.

4. TURN the band down, pulling snugly over the base; wrap to the underside, and staple or tack securely at the centers of the sides.

5. STAPLE the welting to the lower edge, if desired, following tips on page 48; place the welting seam even with the edge of the base. Attach the dustcover as in step 12, opposite.

RED JACQUARD FABRIC GIVES THIS TUFTED OTTOMAN A RICH, CLASSIC LOOK.

TUFTED OTTOMAN

This sturdy, tufted ottoman would be a very useful, decorative piece of furniture for any home. By constructing the frame and upholstering it with your choice of fabric, you can create this beautiful footstool at a fraction of the cost of a ready-made, comparable item. The frame is easy to cut and assemble, using basic carpentry skills and tools. Tufting requires a little practice as you acquire a feel for the fabric. Have patience and give it a try. You will be pleased with your results.

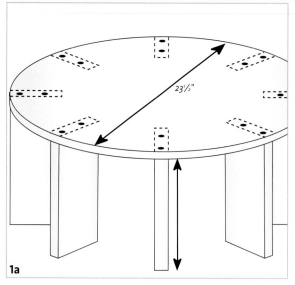

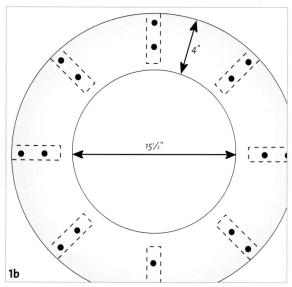

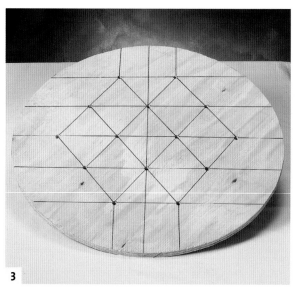

1. FROM 1/2" (1.3 cm) plywood, cut two circles, each 23 1/2" (59.7 cm) in diameter. On one piece, draw a circle 4" (10.2 cm) from the outer edge. Drill a hole large enough to fit the blade of the saber saw inside the inner circle. Using the saber saw, cut out the inner circle. This will be the ottoman bottom. Discard the inner circle. Draw pencil lines across the full circle, dividing it into eight equal wedges. Transfer the marks to the lower ring.

2. APPLY wood glue to the end of one 1 x 4 support. Center the support over one of the marked lines, aligning the narrow edge to the outer edge of the circle. Secure the support with two 2" (5.1 cm) sheetrock screws inserted from the top of the circle. Repeat for each of the remaining seven supports. Then turn the top over and attach the bottom ring to the supports in the same way. Make sure the supports are straight and centered on the marked lines.

3. TO MARK the diamond-tufting pattern on the top of the ottoman frame, draw lines dividing the circle in half vertically and horizontally. Mark a line 3 1/2" (8.9 cm) above and below the horizontal line; mark two more lines 3 1/2" (8.9 cm) above and below these lines—five horizontal lines in all. On the centerline, mark points 2 1/2" (6.4 cm) and 7 1/2" (19.1 cm) from the center. On the first lines above and below the center, mark points 5" (12.7 cm) from the center. On the top and bottom lines, mark points 2 1/2" (6.4 cm) from the center. Draw diagonal lines connecting the points, as shown. Drill 3/8" (1 cm) holes at the marked points and in the two locations shown on the vertical line—14 holes in all.

HOW TO UPHOLSTER A TUFTED OTTOMAN

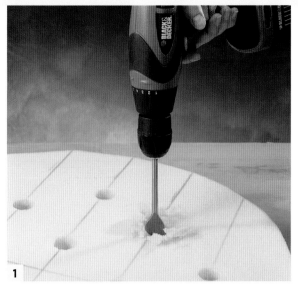

1

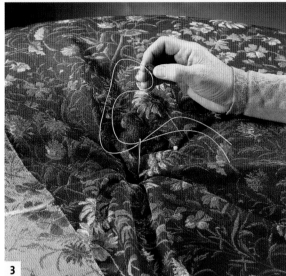

3

2

4

1. MARK a 24" (61 cm) circle on the 3" (7.6 cm) foam. Using an electric knife with the blade held straight up and down, cut out the circle. Mark out the same button placement pattern on the top of the foam circle. Using a 1" (2.5 cm) spade bit and a light touch, slowly drill holes straight down through the foam at the marks. Place the foam over the ottoman frame top, aligning the holes.

2. CUT a 27" (68.6 cm) square of upholstery batting, and center it over the foam. Cut upholstery fabric 45" (114.3 cm) square. On the wrong side, mark a chalk line across the center in both directions. Place the fabric faceup over the batting, aligning the centers and lines. Working on the center horizontal line, flip back the fabric and cut a small hole in the batting directly over the first hole from the center.

Insert a pin through the fabric and batting at the location of the hole on the other side of center, to keep the layers from shifting. Turn the fabric back into position. With a finger, push the fabric down through the batting and into the foam hole to the wood. Wiggle a little slack into the fabric, drawing from the outer edge of the fabric, while keeping the centerlines aligned.

3. THREAD 24" (61 cm) of nylon button twine through the shank of a button. Thread the ends through a button needle.

4. PUSH the needle through the fabric and through the hole in the wood. Pull the twines tight so the button rests against the wood. On the underside of the ottoman top, staple the twines three times as shown.

continued on next page

5

6

7

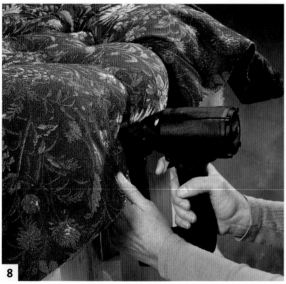

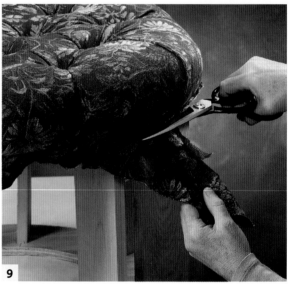

8

9

5. Cut a hole in the batting over the next hole on the centerline. Push the fabric down into the hole as in step 2, and repeat steps 3 and 4. Then do the same for the two holes in the same row on the other side of center. Check to see that the fabric is not pulled too tightly into any of the holes. Release the staples and adjust if necessary.

6. Apply the buttons in each horizontal row, completing each row above center and then each row below center, always working in the holes from the center out. Wiggle slack into each hole, drawing fabric from the outside to prevent pulling the fabric too tightly.

7. When all the buttons are in, use a regulator to turn all the pleats between buttons in the same direction. The pleats should open out just before they reach the buttons.

8. Smooth the fabric over the edge. Beginning at the center front (on a side that has only two buttons), pull the fabric down in a straight line and staple to the edge of the wood circle. Repeat on the opposite side. At the ends of the center horizontal row, pull the pleats straight down over the edge and staple them in place. As you work around the ottoman, pull the pleats straight out to the sides, and then ease in other fabric fullness between pleats.

9. Finish stapling fabric all around the edge. Check to see that pleat lines are straight and fullness is evenly distributed. Trim off excess fabric.

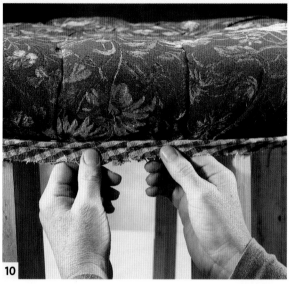

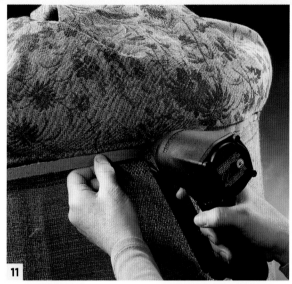

10

11

12

13

14

10. PREPARE welting as on page 46. You will need about 82" (208.3 cm). Wrap the welting around the ottoman over the staples and mark where the ends meet. Finish sewing the welting into a circle. Slide the welting ring back onto the ottoman to check the fit. Remove the welting.

11. CUT fabric for the band 17" x 82" (43.2 x 208.3 cm). Piece the band as necessary. Stitch the welting to the upper edge of the band. Turn the band inside out and, with welting at the bottom, pull it over the top of the ottoman until the welting rests just above the top of the wood. Staple in place using $^1/_2$" (1.3 cm) staples. Wrap burlap around the ottoman and staple in place along the edges of the top and bottom circles. Staple the overlapping ends to the edge of a support. Place a cardboard tack strip over the welting seam allowance with the upper edge even with the stitching line. Staple diagonally through the tack strip.

12. CUT batting 15" x 80" (38.1 x 203.2 cm). Wrap the batting around the ottoman with 1" (2.5 cm) extending above the tack strip. Staple the batting along the tack strip and along the lower edge.

13. TURN the band down and stretch the fabric to the underside of the ottoman. Staple in place using $^3/_8$" (1 cm) staples. Staple at the four center marks first. Then work out the excess fullness as you finish stapling the rest of the band in place.

14. CUT a 27" (68.6 cm) circle of cambric. Turn under the edge and staple it to the underside of the ottoman. Attach four glides to the underside of the ottoman, evenly spaced and 1" (2.5 cm) from the edge.

OVERSTUFFED CHAIR

The upholstery techniques used for an overstuffed chair are commonly used for many other pieces of furniture. The term overstuffed simply means that the chair frame is completely covered with padding and fabric. The instructions that follow are a general guide for upholstering overstuffed chairs. Because styles and design details vary greatly, it is also necessary to refer to the notes, sketches, and photos taken while stripping your particular chair.

This chair is a simple style with an edge wire coil spring seat under a square cushion. Originally the chair had a boxed cushion; however, a new waterfall cushion was made, echoing the rounded curves of the back and arms.

Because there was extensive deterioration to the webbing and spring system, it was necessary to strip the chair to the frame in the seat area. The padding in the arms and back, however, was in good shape, so the remaining upholstery cover was loosened but left intact while working on the seat.

Begin the project by measuring all the chair parts and recording their measurements. Then determine the cut sizes of all the parts, and diagram the fabric layout (page 22). Strip the chair (page 25) as far as necessary. Loosen the lower edges of the inside arms and inside back, and staple-baste the lower edges to the rails to hold them in place. Check the frame for sturdiness and make any necessary repairs (page 26).

At right is a list of the materials that may be needed to reupholster a chair of this type. Depending on the condition of the chair, some existing materials, such as webbing or cushion foam, may be reused.

YOU WILL NEED

- Webbing and webbing stretcher
- Edge roll
- 6" (15.2 cm) curved needle
- Spring twine
- Button twine
- #18 nylon thread
- Burlap
- Upholstery fabric
- Denim
- Deck padding
- Cotton batting
- Foam
- Foam adhesive
- Polyester batting
- Welt cording
- Lining fabric
- Staple gun and staples, ³/₈" or ¹/₂" (1 and 1.3 cm)
- 3" (7.6 cm) curved needle
- Flexible metal tack strip
- Cambric, for dustcover
- Cardboard tack strip
- #15 or #17 finishing nails

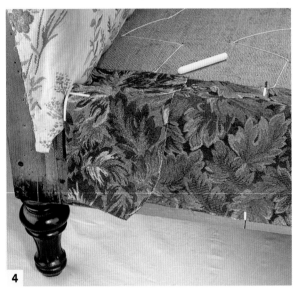

1. CUT a new edge roll, or use the original; position the edge roll, with the flange turned toward the back of the chair and the roll extending ¹/₄" (6 mm) over the burlap-covered edge wire. Thread a 6" (15.2 cm) curved needle with button twine, cut twice the length of the edge roll.

2. INSERT the needle through the front of the edge roll and burlap at the corner, hooking the edge wire and leaving a tail for knotting. Secure the stitch with a slipknot (page 34). Tie an overhand knot (page 35) over the slipknot. Stitch the edge roll to the burlap-covered edge wire, forming lock stitches 1" (2.5 cm) apart. Secure twine at the end of the edge roll with two overhand knots.

3. STITCH the flange of the edge roll to the burlap, using the same knots and stitches used on the front. Run twine under the burlap between stitches. Mark a nosing seam line on the burlap 4" to 5" (10.2 to 12.7 cm) back from the front edge of the edge roll; mark the center of the line.

4. MARK the center top and bottom of the nosing fabric. Pin the nosing fabric to the chair along the marked line, matching centers and extending fabric ¹/₂" (1.3 cm) over the marked line. Fold back the nosing at the outer edges; mark even with the end of the edge roll. Mark again even with the crest of the edge roll. (White tape was used for visibility.)

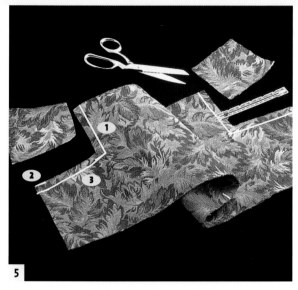

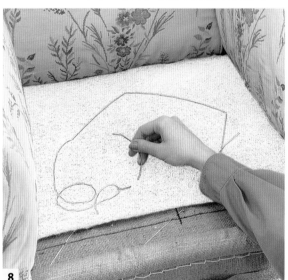

5. REMOVE the nosing fabric. Draw a line parallel to the side from the crest mark to the upper edge (1). Measure the line; mark a point on the side edge a distance from the top equal to the length of the first line (2). Mark another point $^1/_2$" (1.3 cm) below the first mark. Draw a line from the crest mark to the second point (3). Cut out the section, allowing a $^1/_2$" (1.3 cm) seam allowance. Repeat for the opposite side.

6. STITCH a $^1/_2$" (1.3 cm) seam at the corner, curving the stitching line at the fold. Repeat for the opposite corner. Backstitch to secure. Press the seam allowances toward the center. Check the fit.

7. CUT denim for the deck, allowing $^1/_2$" (1.3 cm) for the nosing seam and $1^1/_2$" (3.8 cm) beyond the back and side rails for pulling and stapling. Mark the center front and back. Align the deck to the nosing, matching the center marks; pin. Stitch a $^1/_2$" (1.3 cm) seam, beginning and ending with a backstitch $1^1/_2$" (3.8 cm) beyond the nosing seams.

8. CUT the deck pad to fit the seat, from $^1/_2$" (1.3 cm) behind the nosing seam line, extending 2" (5.1 cm) under the arm rails and back rail; taper the sides as necessary. Stitch the deck pad to the springs with the button twine and curved needle, taking three to five stitches through the burlap; secure the stitches with overhand knots. Cover the deck pad with one layer of cotton batting. Tear edges of the batting; smooth into crevices under the arms and back.

continued on next page

9

11

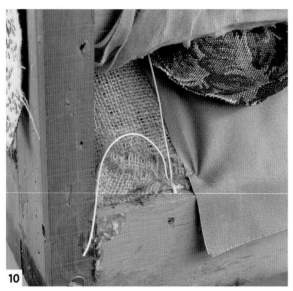

10

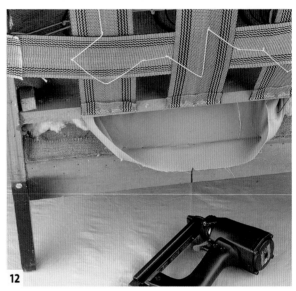

12

9. Lay the deck and nosing over the seat. Fold the nosing back, aligning the seam line to the marked line on the burlap and matching the centers; pin on each side of the center. Pull the seam allowance taut under the arm; staple to the top of the side rail. Repeat for the opposite side.

10. Thread the 6" (15 cm) curved needle with button twine. Insert the needle through the seam allowance and burlap, hooking under the edge wire and exiting on the side of the chair. Staple the end of the twine to the top of the side rail; pull twine in the opposite direction, and staple again to secure.

11. Rethread the needle on the opposite end of the twine. Stitch a seam allowance to the burlap, taking 1" (2.5 cm) running stitches near the seam line; hook springs in the stitches whenever possible. Secure the end as in step 10.

12. Pull the deck under the back. Insert extra cotton between the deck pad and burlap to fill in depressions. Pull the deck to the back rail, matching centers; staple to the top of the rail. Continue stapling the deck to the back rail for several inches (centimeters) on each side of the center.

13

15

14

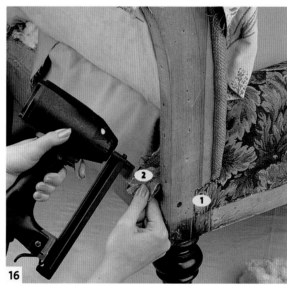

16

13. Cut a strip of deck pad ½" (1.3 cm) narrower than the space between the nosing seam line and the edge roll. Stitch to the burlap, as in step 8. Cover with two layers of cotton batting, torn to the same size. Tear a layer of cotton batting to fit from the nosing seam to the location of the upper band attachment; smooth in place over the other batting and edge roll. Tuck into crevices about 1" (2.5 cm).

14. Pull the nosing straight out and then down, matching the center of the nosing to the center of the front rail. Secure to the face of the rail, stapling several times near the center. Fabric should be pulled snug, but should not compress the front of the spring system. Smooth the nosing down over the padding across the entire front. Staple to the face of the front rail as far as possible. Measure for consistent height from the work surface.

15. Mark a cutting line for fitting around the arm post, as shown; the depth of the Y-cut (page 69) should equal the thickness of the arm post. Cut on the marked lines.

16. Pull the nosing down toward the side. Add padding as necessary. Staple the cut edge to the face of the rail at the base of the arm post (1). Finish stapling the nosing bottom to the face of the front rail. Push the side nosing under the arm to the side of the chair. Pull taut; staple to the top of the side rail (2).

continued on next page

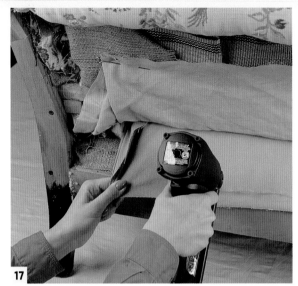

17. ADD padding as needed between the deck pad and the burlap, along the sides of the deck. Pull the deck fabric straight out under the arm, and then downward toward the back. Fabric should be taut but should not compress the springs. Staple deck sides to the top of the side rails to within 5" (12.5 cm) of the back leg post.

18. CUT diagonally into the back corner of the deck, allowing fabric to straddle the back post (page 69); repeat for the opposite corner. Push the deck corner under the back and arm; pull taut on either side of the back post. Turn under the cut edges; staple to the top of the rails. Trim excess deck fabric even with the top edge of the rails

19. STITCH welting to the top of the band; turn the seam allowance toward the band. Place the band on the front rail; flip the band up over the welting. Place a 1/2" (1.3 cm) tack strip over the seam allowance, with the upper edge of the strip just under the seam line. Staple through the tack strip, securing the upper edge of the band; begin at the center and work toward the ends. Place a layer of cotton batting over the front rail, extending batting 1" (2.5 cm) above the tack strip.

20. PULL the band down; staple it to the underside of the front rail, beginning at the center. The batting forms a double layer over the tack strip. Clip the fabric to the lower edge of the front rail at the leg. Fold under the fabric even with the lower edge; staple the ends to the face of the arm posts.

HOW TO UPHOLSTER INSIDE ARMS

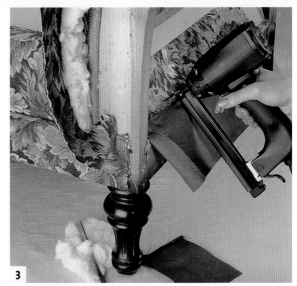

1. REMOVE the cover fabric from the inside arm. Check the condition of the padding, foundation fabric, and webbing. If the webbing or the foundation fabric must be replaced, carefully remove the padding, keeping the original shape intact. Replace any necessary parts; replace the padding. Remove any soiled batting; replace with new batting. Add a new layer of batting, as necessary.

2. LAY fabric over the inside arm, aligning the grain line. Check to see that ample fabric extends to the front and back of the arm. Measure the chair from the outer corner of the nosing to the base of the arm post (1). Smooth the fabric into a crease at the outer edge of the deck. Measure the same distance from the crease toward the lower edge; mark. Draw a cutting line from the mark to the lower edge; draw a Y-cut with the width same as the arm post . Cut on the marked line.

3. SEPARATE fabric at the cut; pull the fabric down, straddling the arm post. Staple to the front arm post and behind the arm post on top of the side rail. Pull the bottom edge of the arm fabric over the side rail; staple to the top of the rail to within 8" (20.3 cm) of the back rail. Pull the top edge of the arm fabric over the top of the arm. Staple once at the center of the outer surface of the arm rail.

4. MEASURE from the point where the inside arm meets the back to the arm stretcher post or the back post just below the top arm rail. Mark a point this distance from the back edge on the horizontal grain of the fabric. Measure again just above the arm stretcher rail; mark. Draw a cutting line from each point to the back edge; the depth of Y-cuts should equal the thickness of the arm stretcher post or the back post. Cut on the marked lines.

continued on next page

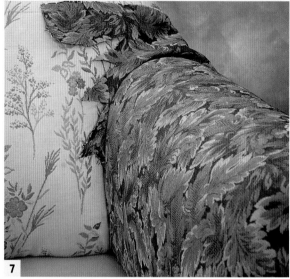

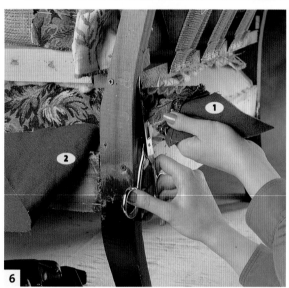

5. PULL the fabric through to the outside; staple the section between cuts to the arm stretcher post, if any. If there is not an arm stretcher post, as in this chair, pin the fabric temporarily to the arm webbing. The section will be permanently attached to the side of the back leg post after the inside back is attached.

6. CUT the lower corner diagonally to the point where it must straddle the back leg post. Pull the section above the diagonal cut (1) to the inside of the back leg post; fold under the cut edge, and staple. Trim excess fabric. Leave open at the back of the side rail (2). The section will be finished after the inside back is attached.

7. MAKE a short relief cut (page 69) off the original cut at the upper back curve of the arm; make additional cuts as necessary to mold the fabric over the curve, making each cut off the one that precedes it. Trim the fabric as necessary. Turn under the flaps of fabric; pull the fabric snugly into a crevice. Staple near the top back corner of the arm rail.

8. STAPLE the back of the inside arm to the side of the back post, clipping and forming pleats as necessary. Finish stapling fabric to the outer surface of the arm rail from center to back.

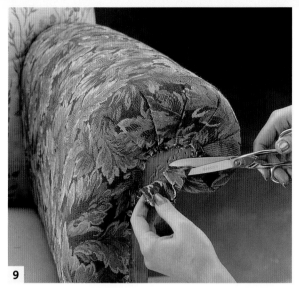

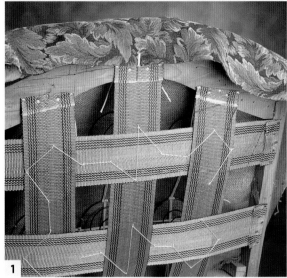

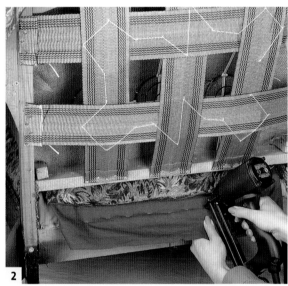

9. PULL the front inside arm down, forming a fold over the nosing; staple. Pull the fabric taut across the arm front, and staple, keeping the grain parallel to the lower edge and working upward to the point of the first pleat. Trim the fabric up to the top staple. Form a pleat, using the flat end of the regulator; staple over the fold. Trim excess fabric. Repeat around the entire curve, spacing pleats evenly.

10. FINISH stapling the underside of the wrapped arm to the outer surface of the arm rail; clip to the rail as necessary. Check for a tight, smooth fit. Release the staples in the top of the side rail; restretch and restaple the fabric. Repeat steps 1 to 10 for the opposite arm.

1. REMOVE all staples and tacks holding the inside back. If the foundation needs repair, remove padding with the cover to keep the padding intact. Retie the springs and apply new burlap, if necessary. Replace the cover and padding; remove the cover. Replace or supplement padding as necessary. Place fabric over the inside back; align the center marks. Staple-baste at the center on the back of the top rail.

2. PUSH fabric through the crevice between the back and the deck. Pull taut; staple at the center of the back rail. Continue to pull and staple fabric for several inches (centimeters) on each side of the center. Pull and staple the upper edge, working outward from the center, until the fabric cannot be controlled without pleats.

continued on next page

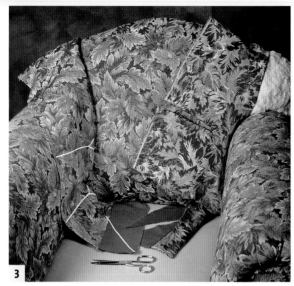

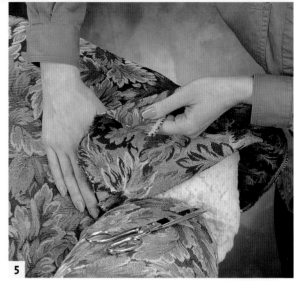

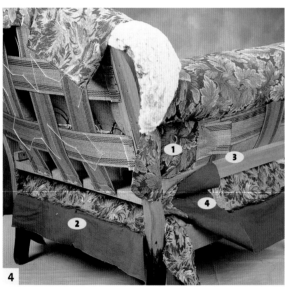

3. MEASURE the distance from each back deck corner to back leg points on the inside back fabric. Mark for diagonal cuts from the corners of fabric; cut. Measure the distance from the intersection of the back and inside arm to the back post at the top arm rail and again at the arm stretcher rail, on each side. Mark these points on the inside back fabric. Mark for a Y-cut horizontally from the outer edges of fabric to each point. Cut.

4. PULL the fabric section through the space between the top arm rail and the arm stretcher rail. Pull taut; staple to the inner surface of the back leg post (1). Separate fabric at the diagonal cut, allowing the fabric to straddle the back leg post. Pull the fabric taut and finish stapling to the top of the back rail (2) and the top of the side rail (3). Finish stapling the lower back edge of the inside arm to the top of the side rail (4), where it was left open from step 6 on page 134. Trim excess fabric.

5. MAKE a short relief cut (page 69) off the upper Y-cut where the inside back wraps over the arm; make additional relief cuts as necessary to mold the fabric over the curve, making each cut off the one that precedes it. Trim the fabric as necessary; turn under the flaps of fabric. Pull the fabric snugly into a crevice and toward the back of the chair. Staple to the back of the back leg post, working upward until the fabric cannot be controlled without pleats.

6. PLEAT out the fullness on the upper corner, as on page 135, step 9. Work upward from the side to the top. Repeat for the opposite side, turning the pleats in the opposite direction and spacing pleats to match the first side. Trim excess fabric at the upper and side edges.

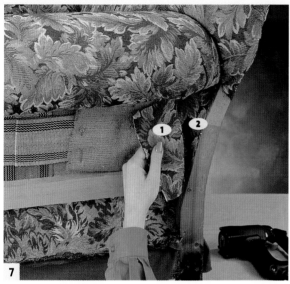

7. REMOVE pins folding the inside arm flap (1) to the webbing. Pull the fabric taut, and staple to the inner surface of the back leg post, over the inside back fabric (2).

8. CHECK the arm and back padding around the deck and along the inside back edges, making sure that both sides are padded equally and without gaps. Add padding as necessary, inserting the padding from the back and sides of the chair. Make any final adjustments necessary in the tautness of the outer fabric. Remove pins holding the arm webbing; staple webbing to the inner surface of the back leg post. Trim excess fabric in areas that have not yet been trimmed. Make the cushion (page 50).

1. PLACE the chair on its side. Mark a line on the underside of the top arm rail in line with the outer surfaces of the front arm post and the back post. Position the outside arm fabric with the horizontal grain line parallel to the lower edge of the chair; allow at least 1¹/₂" (3.8 cm) excess fabric to extend over the front, back, and lower edges. Mark the upper edge, even with the line on the rail; mark the centers on the rail and fabric. Trim the upper edge ¹/₂" (1.3 cm) above the marked line. Cut the lining, using the outside arm piece as a pattern.

2. PLACE the outside arm fabric, facedown, over the roll of the inside arm, aligning the marked line on the fabric to the marked line on the rail. Place the lining over the fabric, aligning the edges; staple-baste within the ¹/₂" (1.3 cm) allowance. Place a cardboard tack strip over the ¹/₂" (1.3 cm) allowance, aligning the outer edge to the marked line. Staple through the tack strip and the fabrics, stapling diagonally near the outer edge of the strip.

continued on next page

3. SMOOTH the lining down taut over the outside arm. Staple to the outer surface of the side rail, front arm post, and back post. Trim just inside the outer edges. Place a half layer cotton batting over the outside arm, extending 1" (2.5 cm) beyond the outer edge of the tack strip. Tear even with the frame edges on the bottom, front, and back.

4. PULL the outside arm fabric down taut over the padding. Staple to the underside of the side rail at the center; continue stapling to within about 4" (10.2 cm) of the front and back legs.

5. CLIP into the fabric as necessary on the curve of the arm. Pull the fabric taut, and staple to the face of the front arm post. Clip fabric to the lower edge of the side rail behind the front leg. Fold under the fabric even with the lower edge of the side rail; pull taut across the front of the leg. Staple to the front arm post.

6. PULL the upper edge of the outside arm around the back rail; staple. Clip fabric to the lower edge of the side rail in front of the back leg. Fold under the fabric even with the lower edge of the side rail; pull taut around the back leg. Staple to the back post. Finish stapling the outside arm along the back post and underside of the side rail. Trim excess fabric.

7

8

9

10

7. ATTACH welting to the outer edges of the back, following the straight lines and curves established by the chair frame. Attach a cardboard tack strip, if the outside back will be hand-sewn. Position the outer edge of strip just shy of the welting seam line. Staple diagonally in the straight areas. Notch the strip for turning the corners; staple parallel to the outer edge in the notched areas. Attach a lining piece, stapling inside the inner edge of the tack strip and even with the lower edge of the back rail; trim.

8. PLACE a half layer cotton batting over the outside back lining. Tear even with the inner edge of the tack strip and the lower edge of the bottom rail. Place the outside back fabric over the batting. Staple-baste to the underside of the back rail to within about 4" (10.2 cm) of the back legs. Clip fabric to the rail at the inner edge of the legs. For attaching the outside back with flexible metal tacking strip, omit steps 9 to 12; follow page 149, steps 12 to 15, attaching continuous tacking strip around the sides and top.

9. TRIM the upper edge near the center to within 1/2" (1.3 cm) of the outer edge of the welt; turn under 1/2" (1.3 cm), and pin. Repeat at the center sides. Then trim the remaining edges to 1/2" (1.3 cm); turn under, and pin.

10. BLINDSTITCH (page 69) the outside back panel to the welting, using a 3" (7.6 cm) curved needle and #18 nylon thread. Knot the end; take the first few stitches into the welt seam line in one upper corner, stitching away from the center to lock the stitches. Reverse the direction; stitch across the top and down one side, spacing stitches 1/2" (1.3 cm) apart.

continued on next page

11. CONTINUE stitching to just above the leg. Fold the fabric under even with the lower edge; stitch to the lower edge. Run the needle through to the opposite side of the welting, coming out at the lower edge of the outside arm. Run thread through the fold over the leg to the front edge of the leg.

12. STAPLE the thread several times to the underside of the side rail, changing direction of the thread with each staple. Repeat steps 10 and 11 for the remaining side of the outside back; secure the thread. Remove the basting staples from the back rail; pull the lower edge taut, and staple to the underside of the back rail.

1. CUT cambric 3" (7.6 cm) larger than the measurements of the bottom of the chair between the outer edges of the rails. Fold under just shy of the outer edge of the rail; staple at the center front, back, and sides. Fold the cambric back at the corner, so the fold is even with the inner corner of the leg. Cut diagonally from the corner of fabric to the fold. Repeat for each corner.

2. FOLD under the cut edges, so folds are tight against the sides of the leg; staple in place. Finish stapling the front, back, and sides, folding cambric under just shy of the outer edge of the rail.

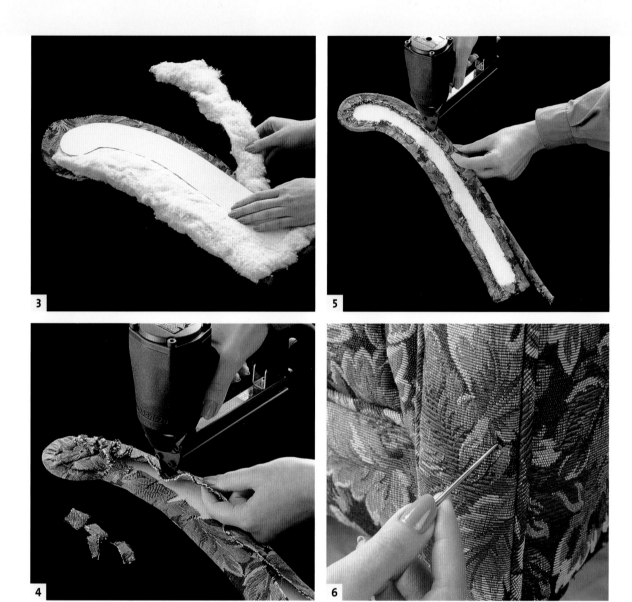

3. Cut fabric for the arm panels 1¹/₂" (3.8 cm) larger on all sides than the arm panel base. Place the fabric facedown on the work surface. Place batting over the fabric; place the arm panel base over the batting. Tear the batting even with the edge of the arm panel base.

4. Pull the fabric taut to the back side of the base, and staple at the centers of the sides and at the top of the curve. Clip the fabric along the inside curve; pull taut, and staple. Pull taut and staple around the outer curve, easing in fullness. Pull taut and staple at the bottom edge. Pleat out excess fabric at the bottom corners; staple.

5. Staple welting to the outer edge, beginning and ending at the bottom of the sides. Follow the tips on page 48. The outer edge of the base should just cover the welting seam line on the front of the arm panel.

6. Separate the threads of the weave to make a hole for a nail, using the point of the regulator (page 11). Insert a #15 or #17 finishing nail; drive into the arm. Insert additional nails as necessary. Close the holes in the weave after driving in the nails. Inspect the chair. Adjust the padding as necessary, using the regulator. Steam the chair (page 68).

LAWSON-STYLE CHAIR

A Lawson-style chair is identified by its boxed arms, boxed and buttoned back, and simple lines. The padding is minimal, cushioning the corners of the arms and back, but allowing the lines to remain rather sharp. Depending on the chair's age, the support in the deck and back may consist of sinuous springs (page 33) or, as with the deck and lower back of this chair, an enclosed manufactured coil spring system.

The nosing of this chair has a hard edge, cushioned by an edge roll that is attached directly to the front rail. The deck is then prepared in a manner similar to that for the overstuffed chair, but without the corner darts.

Much of the outer cover of a Lawson-style chair is sewn together before it is attached to the frame. On this particular chair, the top arms, front arms, and front band are cut as one piece and sewn with welted seams to the inside arms, outside arms, and nosing of the chair. The nosing is hand-sewn to the deck, and then the entire unit is placed over the lightly padded frame and secured. Because the fabric must slide over the batting in the fitting process, polyester batting is recommended.

Begin the project by measuring all the chair parts and recording their measurements. Then determine the cut sizes of all the parts, and diagram the fabric layout (page 22). Strip the chair (page 25) as far as necessary. Loosen the lower edges of the inside arms and inside back, and staple-baste the lower edges to the rails to hold them in place. Check the frame for sturdiness, and make any necessary repairs (page 26). From the materials list at right, select items that will be necessary for your project, depending on the condition of existing materials.

YOU WILL NEED

- Upholstery fabric
- Welt cording
- Polyester batting
- Webbing and webbing stretcher
- Spring twine
- #18 nylon thread
- Burlap
- Edge roll
- Deck pad
- Denim for deck cover
- High-resiliency foam in desired thickness
- Foam adhesive
- Staple gun and staples, ³/₈" and ¹/₂" (1 and 1.3 cm)
- Lining fabric, such as lightweight, inexpensive upholstery fabric
- Button twine
- Buttons
- Button needle
- Cardboard tack strip
- Flexible metal tacking strip
- Cambric, for dustcover

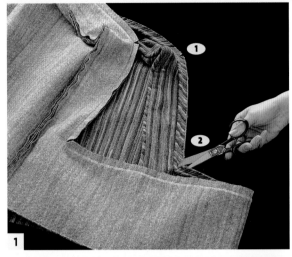

1. STITCH welting to the front and top edges of the outside arm panel. Stitch boxing to the front and top of the outside arm, aligning the lower edge of the front boxing to the lower edge of the outside arm. Repeat for the opposite arm. Stitch welting to the remaining edge of the boxing and the front band. Mark seam allowances of the boxing directly across from the top front corners of the outside arms (1). Clip the seam allowances at the upper corners of the band (2).

2. STITCH the inside arm to the boxing, aligning the mark on the boxing to the top front corner of the inside arm. Backstitch at the clip. Repeat for the opposite arm. Center nosing on the front band. Stitch nosing to the front band between clips, backstitching at the clips. Stitch the deck to the nosing, matching centers. Mark a placement line for a nosing seam on the spring cover; mark the center. Mark the center of the nosing seam allowance. Attach the deck as on page 130, steps 9 to 13, omitting references to edge wire and covering nosing with one layer of batting. Add a half layer of batting from the nosing seam to the lower edge of the front rail.

3. REPLACE webbing on the inside arm, if necessary. Cover the inside arms with burlap. Attach burlap to the outside arms, leaving unattached along the lower edge and for a short distance at the lower front and back. Supplement or replace padding on arms as necessary. Turn the arm cover inside out; position the front boxing in place over the arm front. Turn the arm cover right side out; smooth in place over the chair arm, turning the welted seam allowances toward the inside and outside arm panels. Repeat for the remaining arm.

4. CUT a straight Y-cut on the side edge of the nosing, parallel to the front edge, allowing fabric to fit around the front arm post; the front point of the Y-cut is aligned to the nosing seam line. Pull the nosing down to the front and side, straddling the front arm post with the opposite sides of the Y-cut (1 and 2). Pull taut; staple. Finish stapling the nosing and deck to the top of the side rail. Repeat for the opposite side.

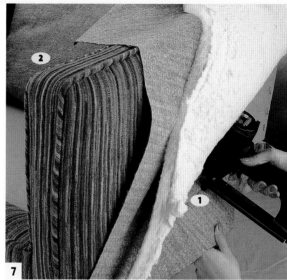

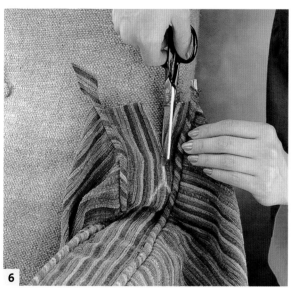

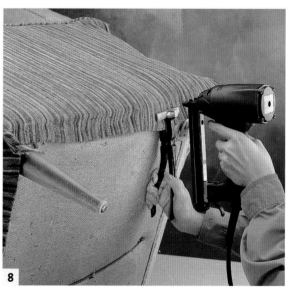

5. PULL the front band taut; staple to the underside of the front rail for several inches (centimeters) at the center. Cut diagonally into the lower front edge of the inside arm, allowing the fabric to fit around the front arm post. Fold under the cut edge of the inside arm from the corner of nosing to the point of the cut (1); pull the lower edge of the inside arm under the arm stretcher rail.

6. CUT a Y-cut in the boxing at the back top of the arm, allowing fabric to fit around the back post. Cut a second Y-cut on the back edge of the inside arm, allowing the fabric to fit around the back stretcher rail. Fold under the edges of the Y-cut on the boxing. Pull the inside arm through to the back of the chair. Pull taut; staple to the inner side of the back rail.

7. PULL the lower edge of the inside arm taut to the side rail (1), pulling the welting along the upper arm slightly to the inside (2). Staple the lower edge of the inside arm to the top of the side rail.

8. PULL the outside arm taut, realigning the welting along the top of the arm. Staple the lower edge to the underside of the side rail, up to within several inches (centimeters) of the back corner. Staple the back edge to the outside of the back post, leaving unattached several inches (centimeters) from the top and bottom. Finish stapling the front band to the underside of the front rail.

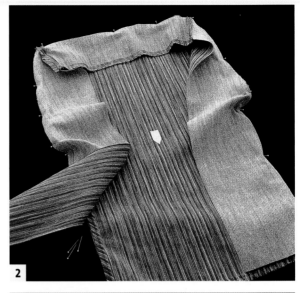

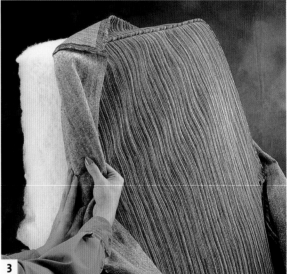

1. PLACE the rectangle of fabric for the inside back over the existing inside back, cutting shallow relief cuts (1) to fit around the arms; pin. Mark a seam line around the outer edge, using chalk. Cut out the inside back ½" (1.3 cm) beyond the marked seam line. Cut the top back boxing to the same width as the upper cut edge of the inside back, with the length of boxing equal to the finished length of the existing boxing plus 2" (5.1 cm). Cut boxing for the sides of the back to the same size as the existing boxing, allowing ½" (1.3 cm) seam allowances on edges that adjoin the inside back and a 1½" (3.8 cm) pulling and stapling allowance on the edge that gets pulled to the back of the chair.

2. STITCH welting to the outer edge of the inside back, avoiding any welting seams on the top of the back. Stitch the top back boxing to the side back boxing pieces, using ½" (1.3 cm) seams; press open. Pin boxing to the inside back, right sides together, matching boxing seams to the top corners. Stitch, using a welting foot or zipper foot.

3. REMOVE the existing back cover. Supplement or replace the padding as necessary. Place the back cover, inside out, over the padding. Turn the cover right side out, fitting the corners snugly; smooth in place over the chair back, turning the welted seam allowances toward the inside back. Pull taut; secure to the outside of the top back rail at the center.

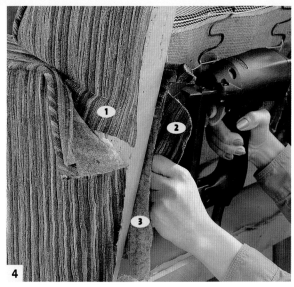

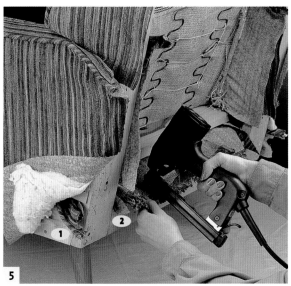

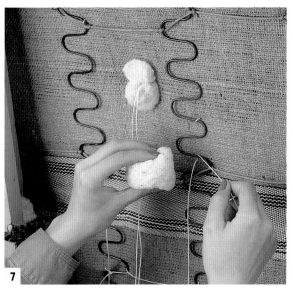

4. CUT a horizontal Y-cut in the side boxing, allowing the fabric to fit around the top arm rail and arm stretcher rail. Pull taut, pulling boxing above the top cut to the outside of the back post (1) and boxing between cuts to the inside of the back post (2); staple over the inside arm fabric (3).

5. CUT the boxing along welting seams at the lower edge of the inside back, allowing the fabric to straddle the back leg post. Pull the welting taut; staple to the top of the side rail (1). Pull the remaining lower edge taut; staple to the top of the back rail (2).

6. FINISH pulling and stapling boxing to the back of the back posts and top rail. Pull the top of the outside arm taut over the inside back; staple to the back of the back post. Finish stapling the outside arms under the side rails.

7. PIN-MARK positions of buttons on the inside back. Cut button twine about 25" (63.5 cm) long for each button. Insert one end of the twine through the button shank; then insert both ends through the eye of the button needle. Insert the needle through the chair back at one pin mark. Pull twine through until the button shank enters the fabric. Separate twines at the back of the chair, straddling a spring, if possible. Tie the twines around a wad of batting, using a slipknot (page 34).

continued on next page

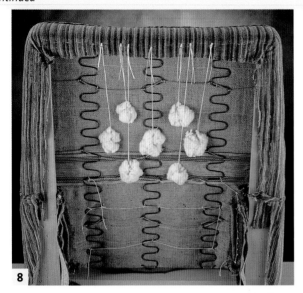

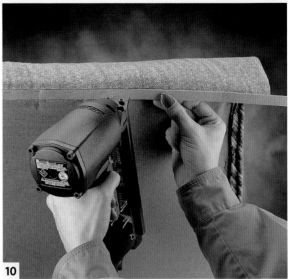

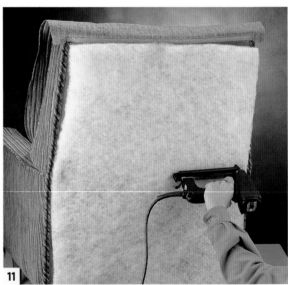

8. REPEAT step 7 for each button. Tighten all of the knots equally, checking indentations of the buttons on the inside back. Secure knots with overhand knots. Pull twines taut to the top rail; staple securely. Make any final adjustments necessary in tautness of the outer fabric. Trim excess fabric in areas that have not yet been trimmed. Make the cushion (page 50).

9. ATTACH welting to the outer edges of the back sides and top, beginning and ending at the bottom of the back rail. Encase cording at the ends as on page 48, step 1. Attach lining to the back, trimming even with the cut edge of the welting. Place the outside back fabric over the outside back. Trim to size, allowing a ¹/₂" (1.3 cm) excess along the top, 1" (2.5 cm) along the sides, and 1¹/₂" (3.8 cm) along the bottom.

10. FLIP the fabric up over the back of the chair. Align the cut edge of the fabric to the cut edge of the upper welting, matching centers. Place a cardboard tack strip over the ¹/₂" (1.3 cm) allowance, aligning the outer edge to the welting seam line. Staple across the top.

11. CUT a half layer of batting to fit between the seam lines of the welting at the top and sides and even with the bottom of the back rail. Staple-baste at the top and side centers.

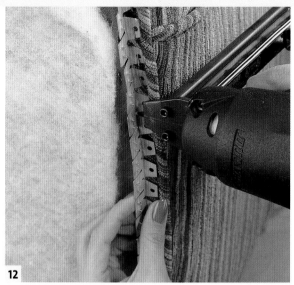

12

14

13

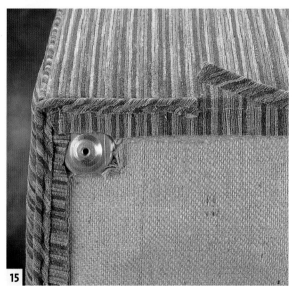

15

12. STAPLE a metal tacking strip to the sides, aligning the outer edge of the tacking strip to the welting seam line. Begin at the upper welting seam line; end at the bottom of the back rail, opening the strip as necessary for ease in stapling. Position the stapler so one leg of the staple goes through each hole in the tacking strip.

13. CLOSE the tacking strip to about 30 degrees. Wrap batting over the edge of the strip to cushion the sharp edge.

14. PULL down the outside back fabric; staple-baste to the bottom of the back rail, matching centers. Trim fabric to ¹/₂" (1.3 cm) along the sides. Tuck the fabric into the tacking strip opening, using a regulator. Push the tacking strip closed along both sides. Hammer the tacking strip securely, using a mallet or tack hammer.

15. PULL the lower edge taut; staple to the underside of the back rail. Attach the welting to the underside of the rails around the bottom of the chair, joining the ends as on page 48, steps 1 and 2. Attach cambric as on page 140, steps 1 and 2.

WING CHAIR

The upholstery steps required for a wing chair include techniques used in both the overstuffed chair and the Lawson-style chair. Wing chairs generally have curved pull-over inside backs, upholstered in the same manner as the overstuffed chair. Close-fitting arms may be boxed and upholstered in a manner similar to the Lawson-style chair, or, as is the case with this chair, the inside arms and front arm panels are sewn together and attached to the chair; the outside arms are attached with metal tacking strips.

Wing chairs usually have a hard edge spring system, which may consist of sinuous springs or coil springs. An edge roll is attached directly to the top of the front rail. The nosing wraps around the front corners of the chair, and the seat holds a T-cushion. Welting defines the lower and outer edges of the wings, the top of the outside back, the front arm panels, and the lower edge of the chair.

Begin the project by measuring all the chair parts and recording their measurements. Then determine the cut sizes of all the parts and diagram the fabric layout (page 22). Strip the chair (page 25) as far as necessary. Loosen the lower edges of the inside arms and inside back, and staple-baste the lower edges to the rails to hold them in place. Check the frame for sturdiness, and make any necessary repairs (page 26).

From the materials list at right, select items that will be necessary for your project, depending on the condition of existing materials.

YOU WILL NEED

- Burlap
- Edge roll
- Upholstery fabric
- Staple gun and staples, $3/8$" or $1/2$" (1 and 1.3 cm)
- Welt cording
- Polyester batting or cotton batting
- Deck pad
- Denim for deck cover
- High-resiliency foam in desired thickness
- Foam adhesive
- Polyester batting
- Mallet
- Lining fabric, such as lightweight, inexpensive upholstery fabric
- Flexible metal tacking strip
- Cardboard tack strip
- Cambric, for dustcover

HOW TO UPHOLSTER A WING CHAIR

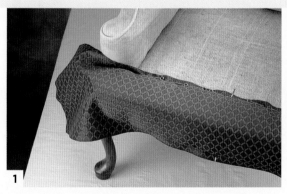

1. Mark a nosing seam line on the burlap 4" to 5" (10.2 to 12.7 cm) back from the front edge of the edge roll; mark the center of the line. Center the nosing fabric faceup over the chair nosing, with the upper edge of fabric extending $1/2$" (1.3 cm) beyond the marked line. Pin along the upper edge. Pull the fabric down over the padding; staple-baste to the underside of the front rail in several places.

2. Fold out the fabric at the front corners to conform to the shape of the chair. Chalk-mark the corner folds.

continued on next page

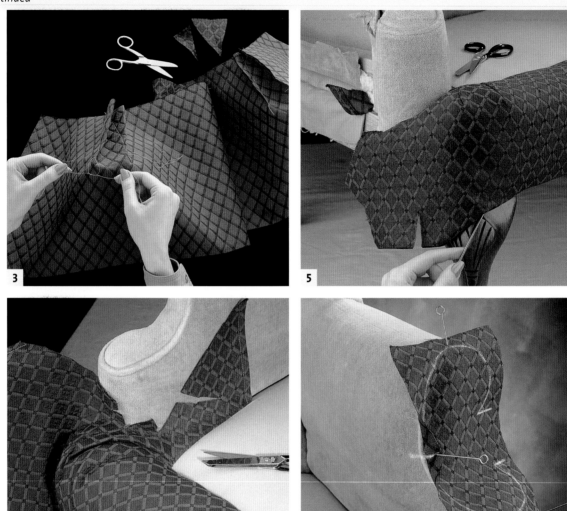

3. REMOVE the fabric from the chair; check to see that the marked folds match corresponding marks on the opposite corner. Stitch folds as marked, back-stitching at the cut edges. Tie threads at the points. Trim to ½" (1.3 cm). Smooth the nosing in place over the chair; check the fit. Adjust, if necessary.

4. STITCH the nosing to the deck fabric, matching the centers; pivot at the corners of the nosing. Attach the deck as on pages 129 to 131, steps 8 to 13, omitting reference to the edge wire in step 10. Pull the nosing down; staple to the underside of the front rail at the center. Cut a Y-cut on each side of the nosing, allowing the fabric to fit around the front arm posts; cut relief cuts (page 69) as necessary.

5. CLIP the lower edge of the nosing just to the bottom of the rail in front of and behind the decorative leg. Turn under the nosing between clips, tucking the fabric under the padding. Pull taut; staple along the fold, if necessary, but only if the lower edge will be finished with welting. Finish stapling the nosing to the front and side rails; finish the deck as on page 132, steps 17 and 18.

6. CHALK-MARK three or more lines for matching around the existing front arm panel, placing two marks at the beginning and end of the welting seam. Place the front arm panel fabric faceup over the front arm panel; chalk-mark the seam line. Transfer matching lines.

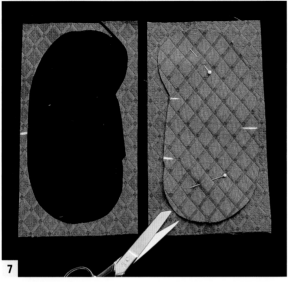

7. REMOVE the fabric; cut out the front arm panel ½"
(1.3 cm) beyond the seam line. Cut a mirror-image
panel for the opposite arm.

8. PLACE the inside arm fabric over the existing inside
arm, wrapping around the front arm post and over
the top arm rail; chalk-mark the seam line around
the front arm panel. Transfer matching lines. Remove
the fabric. Cut out the inside arm around the front
panel, ½" (1.3 cm) beyond the seam line. Cut a mirror
image for the opposite inside arm.

9. STITCH welting around the front arm panel, following the design of the original cover. Pin the inside
arm to the front arm panel, matching the marked
lines; stitch. Remove the old arm cover. Supplement
or replace the arm padding as necessary. Place the
new arm cover, inside out, over the arm, holding the
front arm panel in place.

10. SMOOTH the arm cover back over the arm. Pull taut.
Cut Y-cuts and relief cuts (page 69) as necessary.
Staple the lower edge of the inside arm to the top
of the side rail (1) to within several inches (centimeters) of the back post. Staple the top side edge to
the top arm rail (2). Staple the front side edge to
the outside of the front arm post (3). Check to side see
that the relief cuts and staples at the top back of
the arm (4) will be hidden under the wing welting.

continued on next page

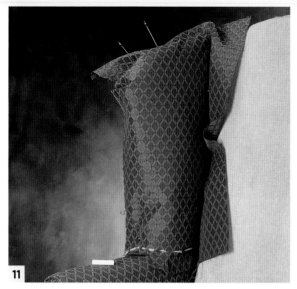

11. PLACE the inside wing fabric faceup over the existing inside wing, aligning the grain lines; pin. Cut shallow relief cuts up to the welting at the lower edge. Chalk-mark the lower welting seam line.

12. REMOVE the fabric. Trim excess fabric ½" (1.3 cm) below the marked seam line. Cut a mirror-image piece for the opposite inside wing. Mark the location of welting on the chair frame; remove the old cover fabric from the inside wing.

13. SUPPLEMENT or replace the wing padding as necessary. Place the inside wing over the padding, aligning the welting to marks on the frame. Pull the welting snug; staple.

14. CUT a Y-cut near the back upper edge of the inside wing, allowing the fabric to straddle the top back rail. Pull the fabric through the crevice between the wing and the back; staple to the inside of the back post.

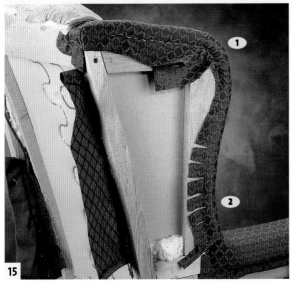

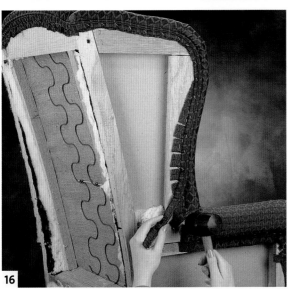

15. Sмоотн the fabric over the front wing post and the top wing rail, wrapping to the outside. Pull taut, and staple, working upward from the welting. Pleat out the fabric as necessary (1); cut relief cuts at the curves as necessary (2). Trim the excess fabric.

16. Uphholster the inside back as for the overstuffed chair on pages 135 to 137, steps 1 to 8, omitting step 5. Attach the welting in one continuous piece to the outside curve of the wings and across the upper back. Flatten the bulky areas with a mallet.

17. Attach the lining and batting to the outside wing as on page 148, steps 9 and 11. Place the outside wing fabric over the batting, aligning the grain line; staple-baste along the outside back rail. Attach the fabric to the welted edge, using a flexible metal tacking strip as on page 149, steps 12 to 14. Release the basting staples at the back; pull taut, and staple. Staple the lower edge to the outside of the top arm rail.

18. Uphholster the outside arm, using a cardboard tack strip along the upper edge and a flexible metal tacking strip along the front edge. Upholster the outside back and finish the chair as on pages 148 and 149, steps 11 to 15; for the curved upper back, use a flexible metal tacking strip instead of cardboard. Trim the seam allowance from the welting where it wraps over the decorative legs.

INDEX

Also Available From
Creative Publishing International

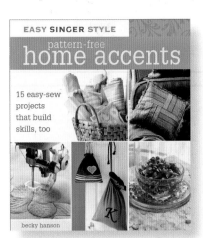

Pattern-Free Home Accents

15 Easy-Sew Projects that Build Skills, Too
by Becky Hanson

To purchase
these or other
Creative Publishing
International titles,
contact your local
bookseller, or visit
our website at
www.creativepub.com

**Singer Simple
Home Décor Handbook**

Essential Machine-Side Tips and Tricks
by The Editors of Singer Worldwide

50 Ways to Paint Furniture

The Easy, Step-by-Step Way to Decorator Looks
by Elise Kinkead

Creative Publishing
international

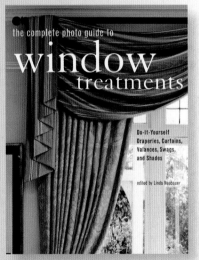

**Complete Photo Guide
to Window Treatments**

Do-It-Yourself Draperies, Valances, and Shades
edited by Linda Neubauer

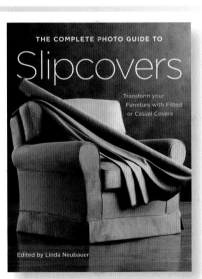

**Complete Photo Guide
to Slipcovers**

Transform Your Furniture with Fitted or Casual Covers
edited by Linda Neubauer